THE ORDER
AND
THE OTHER

Children's Literature Association Series

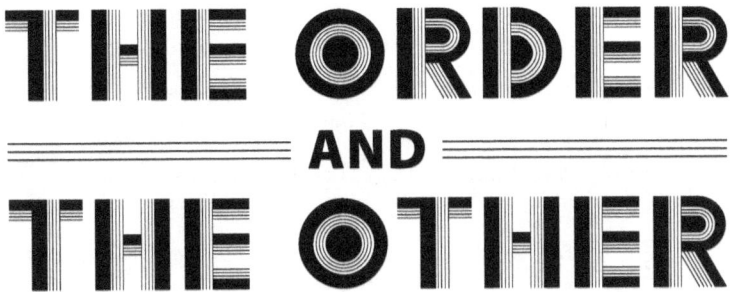

THE ORDER AND THE OTHER

Young Adult Dystopian Literature and Science Fiction

JOSEPH W. CAMPBELL

University Press of Mississippi / Jackson

The University Press of Mississippi is the scholarly publishing agency of
the Mississippi Institutions of Higher Learning: Alcorn State University,
Delta State University, Jackson State University, Mississippi State University,
Mississippi University for Women, Mississippi Valley State University,
University of Mississippi, and University of Southern Mississippi.

www.upress.state.ms.us

The University Press of Mississippi is a member
of the Association of University Presses.

A version of chapter 3 appeared first in the book
Blast Corrupt Dismantle Erase © 2014 from Wilfred Laurier Press.

Copyright © 2019 by University Press of Mississippi
All rights reserved

First printing 2019
∞

Library of Congress Cataloging-in-Publication Data

Names: Campbell, Joseph W. author.
Title: The order and the other : young adult dystopian literature and science
fiction / Joseph W. Campbell.
Description: Jackson : University Press of Mississippi, [2019] | Series:
Children's literature association series | "First printing 2019." | Includes
bibliographical references and index. |
Identifiers: LCCN 2019008117 (print) | LCCN 2019021707 (ebook) | ISBN
9781496824745 (epub single) | ISBN 9781496824752 (epub institutional) | ISBN
9781496824769 (pdf single) | ISBN 9781496824776 (pdf institutional) | ISBN
9781496824721 (cloth : alk. paper) | ISBN 9781496824738 (pbk. : alk. paper)
Subjects: LCSH: Dystopias in literature. | Dystopian films—History and
criticism. | Young adult literature—History and criticism. | Science fiction—
History and criticism.
Classification: LCC PN56.D94 (ebook) | LCC PN56.D94 C36 2019 (print) |
DDC 809/.93372—dc23
LC record available at https://lccn.loc.gov/2019008117

British Library Cataloging-in-Publication Data available

CONTENTS

vii   Acknowledgments

3   Introduction

9   **Chapter 1** | Interpolation, Identification, and the Boundary between Self and o/Other

43   **Chapter 2** | "The Electric Boy Grows Up": Science Fiction for a Young Adult Audience

77   **Chapter 3** | "The Treatment for Stirrings": Dystopian Literature for Adolescents

119   **Chapter 4** | "Teaching the Fantastic": Using Science Fiction and Dystopian Texts in the Classroom

151   **Chapter 5** | "Signs of Life": Considerations for the Future of the Genres and Their Critique

169   Notes

177   Bibliography

185   Index

ACKNOWLEDGMENTS

I first want to thank my mom for sticking with me on this whole crazy ride. Without your support and love none of this would have been possible.

Huge thanks go to Jill, a great friend, and an amazing editor. My writing would not be what it is without your keen eye.

I want to thank Roberta and Melissa because without them, this book wouldn't exist. There is no amount of "thank you" that could ever repay the hours of frustration early drafts of this book put both of you through, but thank you.

I want to thank both Chris and George Jr. for their constant support and for always being up for a theoretical discussion. A lot of the very earliest ideas for this book came from those conversations.

Thank you, also, to Rebecca Bond Costa and Devon Fitzgerald Ralston, Ricia Anne Chansky, Miranda LaBatt, Billie Jarvis-Freeman, Holly Wendt, Melanie Young, Donielle Williams, Diana Quealy-Berge, and Georgia Wheatley for reminding me that someone can engage in theory and yet remain human at the same time.

Thank you, as always, to the Mobile crew, for helping during a very rough time.

Thank you, Dr. Robert Coleman, for putting up with my nonsense, and, Dr. Tom West, for starting this whole thing.

And, finally, a huge thank-you goes out to Katie Keene and all of the fantastic people at the University Press of Mississippi for their diligent work as well as their belief in this book.

THE ORDER
AND
THE OTHER

INTRODUCTION

I believe very strongly that you have to have the right tool for the right job. I was taught this again and again by the men who tried valiantly to train me as a maintenance worker at an apartment complex when I was a young man. They may have failed (because of the poor material that they were working with, not through any fault of their own), but in the end, what they gave me was this foundational understanding: there are many tools that might work for any particular job, and it is up to you to figure out which is the best one.

We can think about literature this way, too. If literature performs critical work, then we might start to think of its various genres and genre characteristics as tools. Part of determining what particular tool goes with which particular job comes from understanding how that tool works, as well as an understanding of the job to be performed.

This is especially true when it comes to the science fiction and dystopian literature, particularly when either is intended for an audience comprised of adolescent readers. One of the maintenance men who tried to train me all those years ago said, "The way you start is by asking yourself what it is you need to do." He meant that I should closely examine the particular job at hand in order to select the right tools for it before starting to work. At one point, the

University of Texas at Austin's College of Education website resource for children's and YA literature called "Books R4 Teens" classified Margaret Peterson Haddix's novel *Among the Hidden* under the category of science fiction, though the novel displays almost none of the conventions of that genre. Likewise, Alleen Nilsen and Kenneth Donelson classify Peter Dickinson's *Eva* as dystopic. I believe that these are misclassifications; I believe that on close inspection, one can see that *Eva* is predominantly a narrative about othering and subjectivity, while *Among the Hidden* is predominantly about power and subjectivity. As I will show later in this chapter, these particular textual trajectories are indicative of a clear orientation toward science fiction in the case of *Eva*, and dystopian literature in the case of *Among the Hidden*. I believe that this sort of misclassification is a result of the fact that dystopian literature is quite often thought of as a subcategory of science fiction. However, science fiction and dystopian literature are not in the same category because they do distinctly different social-critical work in relation to the culture that produces them. This book will establish that it is possible to see the two genres as distinct when they are viewed through the lens of the social critical work they perform, even when some characteristics, such as their settings, may appear to be similar.

In the text that follows, I propose that we, as critics, librarians, and educators, might encourage reading of and/or assign science fiction and dystopian literature that encourages young adults to think critically about and interrogate ways that our culture tries to construct them. Along the way, I am going to show that science fiction and dystopian literature are not the same thing, though very often dystopian literature is classified as a subgenre of science fiction. To me, this particular misclassification is a case of not understanding what the tool in question *does*. I argue this point because helping to understand these tools better, as well as demonstrating the incredibly important work they can do when paired with the right job (i.e., putting them in the hands of adolescents), is extremely important to me. Understanding the concept of othering helps us to understand science fiction, while understanding the interpellating functions of the Ideological State Apparatus / Repressive State Apparatus (ISA/RSA) cycle helps us understand dystopian literature.[1] Ultimately, then, my goal of helping readers recognize and think critically about manipulative discourse so that they will not be manipulated leads to my conclusions about the importance of the use value of genre. It is my hope that furthering an understanding of science fiction and dystopian literature will help others to see how essential it is for adolescents to come into contact with dystopian literature and science fiction and to understand these genres on their own terms.

Over time, science fiction has come to be included as a subgenre of young adult literature no matter the age range the author intended for the text. One colleague was surprised that I wasn't including Frank Herbert's novel *Dune* in this study, as the character Paul is merely fifteen when the novel begins. My rationale is this: though I, too, began my lifelong love of science fiction by reading texts aimed at adults, more and more I see young readers are being directed toward those sections of the library or bookstore set aside for them.[2] In my own forays into bookstores and libraries, I see fewer and fewer young people outside of the area set aside for YA or children's books.[3] While there are reasons that science fiction can legitimately be considered as an adolescent genre no matter the author's or publisher's intent for the text, young readers in the late 2010s are more likely to encounter science fiction and dystopian literature published under imprints intended for young readers and located in the areas of libraries and bookstores set aside for young readers than those located in "adult" areas. Because of this, my focus in this study is on those science fiction and dystopian texts that are branded specifically for adolescents. In other words, this book is not only about the importance of selecting the right tool for the right job, but it is also about examining how the tools that are available determine our perceptions of genre.

In chapter 1, I propose a somewhat stitched-together theory to help create a tool to assist the reader in the exploration of dystopian works. The theory will form a sort of lens through which someone studying dystopian literature in general, but specifically YA dystopian literature, can see how a fictional regime uses rhetorical moves at first, then brute physical power, to form an individual.

In chapter 2, I show in a compressed, somewhat truncated way, the unique history of science fiction. This chapter also shows some of the myriad theoretical approaches that have been used in the study of science fiction over time. I then demonstrate how those approaches have been used by giving close readings of science fiction texts intended for young adults. This is to show the difference between science fiction and dystopian literature. I intend to show that it is a literature directly concerned with the subject's encounter with the other. I believe that, by forcing the audience to see that encounter with the other and the resulting processes of othering more clearly than most realist modes do, the science fiction author asks the audience to be critically aware of those binary constructions.

In chapter 3, I give a history of the utopian/dystopian genre of works over time. This chapter also gives a sampling of theoretical approaches that have been used to study these texts. I specifically show how the theoretical lens I provided in chapter 1 can be applied to these texts, and give specific examples via close readings of dystopian works intended for young adults. I believe that it is a literature intensely interested in providing a clear view of a social model of subject formation (discussed in chapter 1). I feel that dystopian authors are asking their audience to be critically aware of their own ideological constructedness.

In chapter 4, I examine pedagogy related to using science fiction and dystopian works in the classroom. Here, too, there is a specific history that readers may find useful in their own exploration and use of these texts. I also briefly discuss my own experience teaching a class where the goal was to make the very distinction between science fiction and dystopian texts when read side by side that this book is based on.

In chapter 5, I specifically discuss the boom in YA dystopian works that occurred in the 2000s and ask what we are to do now that this boom has come to its end. I briefly touch on current approaches to studying the genre, and suggest further avenues for those who are undertaking an examination of these texts. I then make the case once more for the separation of these two genres.

Thus, this book will show that while in both science fiction and dystopian works the audience is asked to disidentify with the abuses of power that can (and often do) exist in the empirical world, these two different genres engage with power and the individual subject in very different ways. These distinctions are important to note for those who engage with the genres, especially teachers, because what readers look for in texts is largely a function of what we expect from the conventions of the genre that the text occupies.

My goal here is to help people who are interested in studying dystopian literature for young adults to see that genre's roots in the longer history of dystopian literature in general. To see that there is a definition of the word dystopia, which one could use as a general approach in that study, but there is also the specific history of utopian and dystopian texts that have been produced over time; that those texts have specific characteristics; and that understanding the trends in those characteristics will provide an even deeper appreciation of YA dystopian works. In classifying dystopian literature as a subset of science fiction, one might very well wind up looking for characteristics that do not exist in the text and, not finding them, consider the text perhaps flawed in some way. The Los Angeles of *Blade Runner* and the Oceania of *1984* may both be places where we do not want to live, but the points of the stories that we find in those texts are quite different. With that in mind, we can proceed.

Interpellation, Identification, and the Boundary between Self and o/Other

One of the purposes both young adult science fiction and young adult dystopian literature share is to reflect adolescents' own cultural subject formation back to them.[1] This theory exists at the intersection of the works of Louis Althusser, Michel Foucault, and Kenneth Burke. Science fiction, on the one hand, asks adolescent readers to think about who and what they are being asked to other, a concept I will explore more fully later in this chapter, and whether or not they find those binaries to hold true when seen in a new light. Dystopian literature, on the other hand, asks readers to look closely at the ISA/RSA cycle and offers them some sense of agency existing within that system. This cycle of identity formation is based on a central idea of a culturally oriented subject formation. Studying subject formation helps us understand the critical devices employed by science fiction and dystopian literature to create social critique, especially in those texts that work at the intersection of young adult literature and those genres previously mentioned.

One way to study literature is to examine the way texts provide the ideological basis of identification of the individual. I will explore the theoretical basis for a view of subjectivity that is based in post-structuralist thinking, as well as in the reader's interaction with the text, to show both science fiction and dystopian literature function as tools of social criticism, especially in their young adult literature contexts.

The Apparatuses of the State

Althusser's model of ideological transmission from "Ideology and Ideological State Apparatuses" says, "It follows that, in order to exist, every social formation must reproduce the conditions of its production at the same time as it produces, and in order to be able to produce" (86). It is absolutely essential that we understand, Althusser tells us, that any successful society will be one that has come to recognize that, in order to remain a successful society, it must create individuals who believe it important to maintain the society in question. This ideology, along with all the others of a society, then, must be distributed or disseminated. Althusser envisions particular institutional points from which ideology is distributed: the educational system of a particular society, the religious system of a society, the predominant family structure of a particular society, and so forth. He also wants us to pay attention to other institutions, such as the judicial system of a particular society, and the conceptual forms (as well as types of sanctioned actions) of a particular society's policing force(s).

Althusser groups these institutions into one of two categories: those that act mostly by social force (and sometimes on the body) such as educational and religious structures, and those that act mostly on the body (and sometimes by social force) such as policing forces and judicial systems. Althusser calls these groupings the Ideological State Apparatuses and the Repressive State Apparatuses. Althusser tells us that "the Repressive State Apparatus functions 'by violence' [on the body]; whereas the Ideological State Apparatuses function 'by ideology' [power enacted upon the social being]" (97). In other words, ISAs work by transmitting ideology, and RSAs enforce that ideology through means of force enacted on the body, which some interpret as a violence.

We might think of this as a cycle. Envision the various RSAs inscribed as a large circle, and the ISAs inscribed as a circle within the larger RSA circle, with its lines of force flowing inward from the circumference. Thinking of the relationship this way helps us to understand that, should a subject attempt to move outside of the influence of the ISAs (ostensibly by rejecting the socialization processes inherent in interpellation in the Althusserian schema), then he or she finds him/herself in the realm of the RSA—bodily arrested in their movement and forcefully returned to the ISA circle, likely at gunpoint. I believe that it is quite useful for us to envision the ISA/RSA relationship in this way: as a series of interrelated forces acting on the subject. Callinicos summarizes this particular aspect of Althusser this way:

> The category of the subject is therefore uniquely fitted to the purpose of ideology since the complicity of the subject and object that underlines it gives the world a meaning *for the individual* that suppresses the mechanism of exploitation and oppression at the heart of society and the meaningless chaos at its surface. Both are abolished in a system of ideal relationships which picks out each individual, giving him a unique value by virtue of the relation that exists between him and the world under their aspect of subject and object respectively. (65–66)

The subject is offered choices—should he or she or it reject the options given in the sphere of the ISAs, he or she or it becomes the concern of the RSAs. The RSAs will then attempt to move them, bodily, back into the sphere of influence of the ISAs. "Be a subject or else," the RSA tells the subject brought before them. Althusser would have us understand that being a subject to these processes is a function of language. The subject is always-already a subject: "Ideology has always-already interpellated individuals as subjects, which amounts to making it clear that individuals are always-already interpellated by ideology as subjects" (119). Eve Wiederhold shows that

> In an Althusserian view of language, for example, "the call" of language's law is one of interpellation. To be addressed as "a moral citizen" is not merely to be so identified but to invoke linguistic practices that make possible such identifications. We become law-abiding citizens by being interpellated within the terms of a language that makes available the very idea of "citizenship" and "morality." Hence, identifications of "good citizenship" do not reflect an existent essence of "goodness" but draw upon whatever symbols a given culture employs to describe such a quality. (131)

The subject, by the very essence of subjectivity, is an interpellated figure. Because of this, some would say that in an Althusserian view, ontological possibility within such a system is circumscribed. The subject, it would seem, is an endpoint of ideology with very little agency.

To be always-already interpellated, though, makes some feel that free will has been extinguished. Althusser's structures fail in many ways to assign the agency of subjects, positing them as an endpoint to ideology. As Wiederhold explains, this view of Althusserian theory, "implies that any image of self-determined consent is an illusion" (137). Thinking of the subject as merely a point on which ideology acts is a concept that can chafe. Indeed, this rejection will form the primary point of contention to the theory of how interpellation works that I pose, here. This does not mean, however, that we should reject the concept altogether. I believe that this means we should explore it further, so I will do this below.

Another major point of contention many theorists have, however, is with Althusser's seeming abandon of the revolutionary trajectory of the Marxist project. If the subject is merely the endpoint of ideological pressures, where does that leave us? Can the subject transcend ideology? More to the point, if the subject cannot transcend the ideological constructions that create and maintain capitalist modes of production, where does that leave the Marxist project?

Indeed, a predominant theme in the critique of Althusser seems to be his apparent removal of Marxist thought from the struggle of the proletariat against those who control the means of production. McDonnell and Robins feel that "it is totally contrary to the spirit of Marxist method to separate as [Althusser] does, the sphere of reproduction, the domain of the ISAs, from the sphere of production" (166). Simon Clarke feels that the problem is that the project of the Althusserians, as he calls them, reverses what he feels is the proper emphasis of critique. He says that the Althusserian critique, which he thinks of as "utopian socialism," bases

> itself on a *moral* critique of bourgeois relations of *distribution*, and so aiming at the transformation of relations of distribution without any transformation of bourgeois relations of production, the revolution being introduced from outside because of the necessarily moral basis of the utopian critique. (17)

Those who have adopted Althusserian modes of critique take the relations of production to be a given and concentrate instead on critiquing the modes of distribution. It is in this way that Warren Montag believes that Althusser fails to take into account the lived experiences of what he calls "concrete human beings" (55). Even Callinicos, who generally agrees with Althusser, finds himself critiquing Althusser on this point:

> Althusser's approach to the state carries with it the danger of replacing the struggle against the capitalist state by a struggle *in relation to* apparatuses which function to inculcate ideology, *at present* in the hands of the bourgeoisie, but which may be *taken over and used* to inculcate "proletarian" ideology rather than bourgeois ideology. (105)

He asks us to consider the question "where is the sense of the revolution in a critical stance that says the battle is already lost?" If the goal can only be to change the ideologies that are being produced by the machine, and not to destroy the machine altogether, then where does that leave the Marxist struggle? Callinicos says that it is precisely at this point that Marxists must begin the critical debate about Althusser (prefiguring in some ways the very thing that Žižek does). Lovell levels the claim that this Althusserian theoretical critique, abstracted from the Marxist revolution strategic trajectory, leads to lapses. He says,

> More seriously, even the more impressive and substantial contributions to cultural studies from these sources are characterized by difficulties and ambiguities of a fundamental kind. This tendency, or rather, complex of tendencies, has dominated the field of Marxist cultural studies now for a considerable period of time, without having made significant progress toward resolving, or even seriously confronting, these problems. (233–34)

What is the aim of Althusserian critique, then, if it is no longer tied to the Marxist revolutionary trajectory? More to the point, if ideology is always-already existent and enacted in Althusser, where does that leave the field of ideology critique? McDonnell and Robins might say that the goal is to find ways to practically subvert ideology via everyday interventions. They point out that

> ideology is far from watertight; it requires an incessant struggle by the capitalist class to maintain its precarious validity. A validity that is constantly called into question, *not in a separate sphere of ideological struggle, but throughout the daily struggles in the workplace, the community, etc.*—for ideology is an organic and integral part of all social practices. The problem remains, of course, that although it is possible to demystify ideology, one does not thereby change social reality: one is still confronted with the imposing and dominating reality of the "real abstractions." (168)

Althusserian critique, then, can still lead to revolutionary praxis in the sense that it is not always a revolution *en masse* that creates change. Perhaps it is through a million little revolutions each day against *dominant* ideology that progress can be made. Warren Montag says that the dilemma is "how to diminish the forces that individuate and separate us and thus prevent us from uniting with others in order to act and to think more effectively and with greater strength for our liberation. What can liberation mean without transcendence?" (77). It is important, however, to recognize that liberation as freedom from all ideology (a somewhat outmoded concept of liberation's meaning) could not and should not be the goal. A revolution that moves us from the predominant ideological positions that we experience daily into more humane ideological positions within the sphere of the possible can be, though, and should be.

The Normative Gaze

Althusser's ISA/RSA structures are quite useful for describing the ways a subject, in what we might think of as post-mirror-stage, is formed by discourse moment by moment via language. I will be using these Althusserian structures as key elements in a hermeneutic to describe a socialization process via ideology. There is a volitional component to subjectivity in this sense: the social individual has the choice to move within the web of signifiers (or, more to the point, within the space of any signifier except "subject," one which the subject automatically possesses within ideology). Foucault might call this the polyvalent nature of power within the sphere of the social. We might think of these as rhetorically placed signifiers that confer power in various senses, hence what Burke, though prefiguring Foucualt's sense of polyvalent power relations, might call the moves of identification that are so essential to subject formation.

Michel Foucault's overall project is multifaceted. Here, I want to focus in on the part of his work that discusses how power is enacted on bodies (which he calls discipline), and how he analyzes the mechanisms that allow this to occur (such as surveillance). Primary among those mechanisms is the concept of normative surveillance.

Normative surveillance describes the ways that power is enacted on the bodies of subjects in institutions designed to discipline them (mental hospitals, schools, family homes, etc.). Foucault says, "The perfect disciplinary apparatus would make it possible for a single gaze to see everything constantly...a perfect eye that nothing would escape" (173). This is, then, a "disciplinary gaze." The eye he posits is normative (*Discipline* 170–79). Normalization, Foucault tells us, is the aim of power within an institution:

> the art of punishing, in the regime of disciplinary power, is aimed neither at expiation, nor even precisely at repression.... it refers individual actions to a whole that is at once a field of comparison, a space of differentiation, and the principle of a rule to be followed ... it measures in quantitative terms and hierarchizes ... in short, it *normalizes*. (*Discipline* 182–83)

Individuals are always under the gaze of those wielding power in institutions designed to discipline them. These individuals are measured against a set of "norms" (determined ideologically) for deviation—both above the norm and below. It is in this way, Foucault says, that "discipline 'makes' individuals; it is the specific technique of a power that regards individuals both as objects and as instruments of its exercise" (*Discipline* 170). Foucault does not theorize the disciplinary gaze as somehow separate. He says, "The exercise of discipline presupposes a mechanism that coerces by means of observation; an apparatus in which the techniques that make it possible to see induce effects of power, and in which, conversely, the means of coercion make those on whom they are applied clearly visible" (171). All institutions, Foucault tells us, are engaged in the process of normalization of the subjects they contact. Vighi and Feldner sum up Foucault's point quite nicely when they say, "Normalization is the most pervasive form which Power assumes in the modern world" (89). That is, the gaze that is always directed at the individual by those around him or her is watching for transgression against the dominant ideology.

Given this interpretation of one aspect of Foucault's work, a conflation of Foucault with Althusser becomes possible. The notion of discipline being carried out on individuals sounds very much like ideological pressure from the ISAs.[2]

Foucault's sense of power is quite different from Althusser's. Foucault's sense is based in the polyvalent web he speaks of, in which the subject is mobile—for Foucault, power is formative and repressive simultaneously. Althusser's sense of power is that it represses. This is the reason that I intend only to use certain aspects of Foucault's theory in combination with certain aspects of Althusser's work creating, in a sense, a very specific lens to look through. To be more specific, I am using Althusser's sense of the ISA/RSA system, with Foucault's sense of power as it contacts the body as a way of thinking about how the pressures exerted by those ISA/RSA pressures work at the physical level. I use this particular lens because it helps us to see the dividing line between dystopian literature and science fiction more clearly, since I assert that such ISA/RSA pressures being metaphorized within such texts is their primary goal. I also believe that this social constructivist model provides a valuable tool to show ideological construction of the subject to adolescents.

The critics of Foucault, though, are skeptical. Fabio Vighi and Heiko Feldner say that they believe, "Foucauldian theory does not encourage us to ask 'What is power and where does it come from?,' but instead 'How is it practiced?' . . . naïve and essentialist as 'what is' questions might appear, they remain indispensable" (25). Dorrit Cohn believes we may also criticize Foucault on the basis of what the outcome of such power might be. She says, "Modern institutions that supposedly transfix their charges in this manner are not, after all, known to produce uniformly and perfectly obedient and submissive prisoners, students, workers, or sons/daughters" (3–4). Though I take Cohn's point, here, I have to argue that perhaps the idea of perfect obedience is not the end goal of the process—even seeming anarchists still accept subjecthood and the way subjectivity relates to social structures.

Joan Copjec calls Foucauldian theory to task because it does not allow for "any reference to a principle ... that 'transcends' the regime of power he analyses" (qtd. in Vighi and Feldner, 90). Kevin Jon Heller feels we must resist what he calls the "monolithic interpretation" of Foucault's work. He says that again and again, Foucault is misinterpreted as saying, "Power is repression; agency is a myth; subjectification is enslavement; resistance to power is futile; freedom is impossible" (105). Heller feels that this reading is highly selective and does not actually reflect the positions Foucault would recognize as his own work. As Heller points out, "Traces of the self-founding, self-transparent Cartesian ego are nowhere to be found in Foucault's texts; like mechanisms of power, individual subjects are, for Foucault, always produced by a pre-existing system of power-relations—the power-diagram—that makes their existence possible" (91). Many would interpret such a subject to be without power, without agency. However, this would be a misreading of Foucault. As Heller goes on to say, "what [Foucault] is actually arguing is that we must reject the possibility of 'liberated' subjectivity itself, however defined, because any such concept of liberation necessarily depends upon the Cartesian illusion of subjectivity existing outside the process(es) of subjectification" (92).

As Heller also points out,

> Foucault opposes *repressive* subject-positions to *liberated* subject-positions—a judgment which, he is willing to admit, is always made from a partisan and thus contestable perspective—not *ideological* subject-positions to *non-ideological* subject-positions. After all, it is precisely Althusser's idea that subjects are always-already interpellated through ideology that subtends Foucault's own work on the construction of subjectivity. For Foucault, subjects simply *are* their ideologies. (93)

Foucault's conception of power is a multivalent force. It moves in all directions simultaneously. Subjects formed by power are, likewise, moving in all directions simultaneously—acted on by power and enacting power at the same time. For Foucault, "'resistance to power is never in a position of externality to power,' rather, it is 'inscribed in the latter as an irreducible opposite.' Resistance, then, does not predate power but relies on and grows out of the situation against which it rebels" (qtd. in Vighi and Feldner 90). Resistance to power may be an ideological position within a seemingly endless sphere of ideological positions, but that does not mean that it is *merely* an ideological position. Neve Gordon feels that, in his later work, Foucault shifted in his sense of the subject and agency: "The Foucauldian subject has gained agency, yet at the same time it is always situated within a web of constraints, and therefore cannot be conceived as an entity autonomous of power relations and background practices" (413).

The issue of a transcendent "spirit," if you will, is not excluded by his theory, merely *from* it. Instead, we must see Foucault's work as performing a specific type of inquiry that does not concern itself with that issue. He himself says, "Well, rather than worry about the problem of the central spirit, I believe that we must attempt to study the myriad of bodies which are reconstituted as peripheral subjects as a result of the effects of power" (qtd. in Heller 94). Note: "Rather than"—not "instead of." The distinction is important in the way it affects how we view the debate. He does not reject the possibility, but instead notes that an examination of "soul" is outside the scope of his concern.

Cohn asserts that "the panoptic conceit [in literary interpretation] is powerfully charged with negative meaning and invariably contextualized in ideological interpretations" (3). In some ways, I am doing here the very work she is describing. Panopticism may not be the center of my work, but it certainly informs my reading of Foucauldian normative surveillance. Though the scope of my examination will inevitably involve negative instances of normative power being used on the individual in the form of the dystopian novel for young adults, not all instances of power are automatically negative—nor are they always positive.

I intend to use Foucault's sense of an invisible, normative eye as a way to augment an understanding of Althusserian structures. Foucauldian normative surveillance and normative power are the link between the Althusserian ISA and the subject. But, as I said, the subject is without power in this situation. In order to theorize how the subject moves within these power structures (in a sense, pushing back on the power exercised from the social structure) are the movements of identification as theorized by Kenneth Burke.

The Trans-Ideological Kernel

The theoretical work of Slavoj Žižek is extensive in exploring the interactions between culture and the individual using a potent combination of Marxist thought and Lacanian psychoanalysis. In this particular way, Žižek has come to critique late capitalism and the way it works on societies (especially the United States in the early twenty-first century).

Žižek's judgment of Foucault's theory of power and discourses is that, "within the scope of Foucault's theorization of power, where resistance is always-already co-opted in advance, the prospects 'for individuals to rearticulate and displace the power mechanisms they are caught in' are practically zero" (Vighi and Feldner 97). Is the subject "merely" the endpoint of operations of power? Does the subject have any agency in the system at all?

Žižek believes that we might find a refutation to the idea that the subject is only ideology expressed bodily within the concept of subjectivity, itself. His position is that there is still something, some "essence," as he puts it, that does exist outside of ideological construction. It is precisely this trans-ideological kernel, as he calls it, of the subject that exists outside of these constructive discourses that allows ideology to work:

> The lesson is therefore clear: an ideological identification exerts a true hold on us precisely when we maintain an awareness that we are not fully identical to it, that there is a rich human person beneath it ... in every ideological edifice, there is a kind of trans-ideological kernel, since, if ideology is to become operative and effectively "seize" individuals, it has to batten on and manipulate some kind of "trans-ideological" vision which cannot be reduced to a single instrument legitimizing pretensions to power ... *it is only the reference to such a trans-ideological kernel which makes an ideology "workable."* (*The Plague of Fantasies* 21)

There must be, he says, some object that ideology is working upon. In other words, although we may not posit a space outside of ideology, even one from which to be critical of ideology itself (for such a space always-already was ideological, as well), there must be some trans-ideological kernel from which the moves of identification emanate.

Because of this belief, Žižek feels that as we come to understand the trans-ideological kernel, we must not begin to fall back on ideas that there is somehow a space outside of ideology. In using science fiction and dystopian literature for adolescents, we must not find ourselves positing some utopic vision of a place outside the web of power relations (Foucault) or ideological pressure (Althusser) as the end goal. Thus, I try to be extremely careful in examining the ways that literature can function as an intervention into ideological subject formation that we do not posit such intervention strategies as some grand gesture of "freedom."

As Žižek warns us,

> one should be careful to avoid the last trap that makes us slide into ideology under the guise of stepping out of it. That is to say, when we denounce as ideological the very attempt to draw a clear line of demarcation between ideology and actual reality, this inevitably seems to impose the conclusion that the only non-ideological position is to renounce the very notion of extra-ideological reality and accept that all

we are dealing with are symbolic fictions, the plurality of discursive fictions, never reality—*such a quick, slick, "postmodern" solution, however, is ideology* par excellence. It all hinges on our persisting in this impossible position: although no clear line of demarcation separates ideology from reality, although ideology is already at work in everything we experience as reality, we must none the less maintain the tension that keeps the critique of ideology alive . . . it is possible to assume a place that enables us to maintain a distance from [ideology], *but this place from which one can denounce ideology must remain empty, it cannot be occupied by any positively determined reality*—the moment we yield to this temptation, we are back in ideology. (*The Žižek Reader* 70)

To critique ideology from a place that assumes it is outside of ideology is simply ideological positioning once more. Therefore, we must come to understand that the position of critiquing ideology is one more position that is available in the web of positions.

Vighi and Feldner summarize the argument about ideological positioning thusly:

Thus, key to [Žižek's] critique is the question of externality: while the traditional positing of a conceptually viable space outside ideology is delusive, the negation of externality *tout court* is also defective, for it thwarts the articulation of radical political projects. Moving beyond traditional critical theory (where ideology deforms "true" reality) and discourse analysis (where ideology is turned into an all-encompassing discursive practice), Žižek identifies a third model, whereby a place outside Ideology is possible . . . [but] can never be retrieved as a rational paradigm, *and for this very reason (because it relates to a non-discursive core) it is Ideology at its purest.* (37)

The danger is that, in critiquing ideology, we might find ourselves thinking we have somehow freed ourselves from it. This is not false consciousness in the sense that early Marxism used the term, but it is a close cousin. Whenever we are working with ideology critique, this is a danger. "[A]ll we can do, if we do not want to fall prey to the lures of ideology as a privileged-viewpoint theory, is to describe the workings of discourse and power-knowledge" (Vighi and Feldner 27). The consumers of science fiction and dystopian literature are given an opportunity to examine the intersections of the myriad discourses that construct them moment by moment; this is not some attempt to produce a space somehow *outside* ideology for them to occupy.

This very concern is the reason that nowhere in this book will I be engaging in the idea of theorizing a utopic freedom from ideology. I realize that not doing so opens this work to the same critiques leveled against Foucault and Althusser. However, I feel as Meli Steele does when she says, "The reason poststructuralists do not evoke utopian criteria is that they want to avoid the Marxist dialectic of ideology and utopia in which history is viewed as the self-realization of humanity. Such a theory makes presuppositions about human nature and emancipation that are themselves oppressive" (Steele 32).

Moves of Identification

We might think of Foucault's work as a bridge between the ISA and the body in terms of interpellation; if so, then how does the subject move within that web of power? Kenneth Burke's theory is wide ranging but tends to focus on concepts of mankind as a symbol-using animal and how people are affected by their encounters with those symbols. In *Rhetoric of Motives*, Burke explains the functioning of rhetorical movements of unity. He says, "Identification is compensatory to division. If men were not apart from one another, there would be no need for the rhetorician to proclaim their unity. If men were wholly and truly of one substance, absolute communion would be of man's very essence" (22). In Burkean rhetoric, people are divided from people. There exists a space between subjects. Rhetorical moves create the rhetorical identifications to create an "us," a space where that distance between subjects is reduced.

Suddenly, instead of two separate subjects, a "we" emerges due to some rhetorical intervention between speaker/writer and audience. Here, I will describe two specific smaller movements that overlap in the Burkean process of identification as I intend to use it: identification and scapegoating. In Burke's theory, subject A only sees of subject B what the ideology A is interpellated with will allow. Thus, to create a "we," subject A then begins the movement of self that brings him or her to combine with the part of B that he or she can see through that ideology. Burke puts it so, "To identify A with B is to make A 'consubstantial' with B" (20). We must remember, of course, that A does not *become* B: the space does not collapse. Subject A in all actuality becomes something more akin to A(B), with B denoting the part of B's subjectivity that A has come to admire and wishes to emulate. A in some ways wishes to become "simultaneously 'me' and 'not me'" (Ratcliffe 57). In order to accomplish this move, A must excise some part of self, creating an "exiled excess," as Krista Ratcliffe calls it. It is possible for that identification of "non-B-self" to become "unclean self" quite quickly in such a rhetorical ideological environment. Burke's identification system is one in which "identification does provide a place of personal agency and a place of commonality, yet it often does so at the expense of differences. As a place of common ground, Burke's identification demands that differences be bridged" (53). The danger in the move of identification that creates a "we" by excluding a "them" is, of course, that there may be far more similarity between the in-group and those who are shunned than appears on the surface. Instead of difference as something to be celebrated (an orientation toward diversity), it is automatically thought of as something to be overcome.

But what happens if the desire is to further the distance between subjects? Burkean theory of identification fits within another of his theoretical ideas, that of hierarchy. In Burke's concept of the scapegoat, A recognizes some aspect of B that A cannot abide, given the ideology that composes the symbol veil. Negotiation is then forbidden between the two. To attempt to see any part of B that is acceptable would be for A to soil him or herself. This forms a boundary to which A may adhere. It is fairly easy to see that movements of identification likely involve movements of power (in a sense aligning them with Foucauldian thought). As Carter says,

> The ladder of symbolic rank is extended to greater heights and depths. Everyone feels that there are both lower and higher rungs available. Everyone has the opportunity to locate someone toward whom it is possible to enjoy feeling superior. Few are so low that they do not fear slipping another notch. (9)

What might happen to the person that is lowest on that ladder, though? We might think of that individual, the "lowest of the low" in a sense, as what Burke describes as the scapegoat. Burke says that "the scapegoat . . . combines in one figure contrary principles of identification and alienation" (140). The scapegoat is the rhetorical figure that receives the blame for the current state that the "we" created by identification must endure. We might think of the scapegoat as subject C. In this case, then, in identifying with B, subject A is in some ways *dis*-identifying with subject C. The excess that A must exile, in Ratcliffe's terminology, in order to become A(B), leads to a sense of undesirability. C, then, is the subject that most embodies that exiled part of A's self. The boundary that brought the very "we" together in community now divides that community from the figure upon which all the rhetorical scorn of the community is brought. "Our" condition would be better if only "they" were punished, if you will. Or, more to the point, "we" exist because we all agree that we cannot and must not be "like them." Any contact with C, then, would sully AB and could cost him or her that particular rung on the ladder. Somewhat counter to what we may think, though, it is the sacrifice of the scapegoat (exile or, in extreme cases, death) that cleanses the community. In this way, though lowest on the social rung, the scapegoat is powerful—all the transgressions of the community may be heaped upon the scapegoat and purged with their sacrifice.

The Unsacred Man

In many ways, the identificatory and *dis*-identificatory movements of subject A(B) are attempts to avoid becoming what Georgio Agamben would call *homo sacer*, that subject who is stripped of the protection afforded by his/her citizenship (de la Durantaye 200–38). Agamben's work involves two specific concepts coinciding: the state of exception and the human who is so "low" that he or she can no longer be sacrificed. When speaking of the state of exception, what Agamben means is that situation where the sovereign declares that, because there is a threat to safety (to his or her own self or to the society in general), laws may be suspended—including the very laws that protect the lives of the subjects under the sovereign's control. The second concept, that of the unsacred man, *homo sacer*, is the person who, under that state of exception, may be killed, but not sacrificed. The worth of *homo sacer* has fallen so low that killing him or her is no longer considered murder, and she/he is worthless for the purpose of sacrifice.

If Burke's subject A(B) were to transgress those rhetorical/ideological boundaries and become "sullied" by contact with C, she or he might very well have her or his citizenship revoked, leaving him or her open to whatever punishment the culture she or he resides within deems fit to hand out. Worse, because of the transgression (if made public), such treatment at the hands of the RSAs might be applauded by the culture subject A(B) formerly found him or herself within. It is a movement both internally as well as externally motivated in that way. As Karen Coats says in her exploration of Julia Kristeva's thoughts on abjection in regard to the social body, "Just as we abject the unclean and improper evidences of the body's physicality in order to constitute a clean and proper body, so in the social realm we abject the unclean and improper . . . in order to constitute the boundaries of community and nation" (141). The boundary between the subject who submits to social pressure and those who refuse to is something like a type of heavily policed bodily boundary.

Burke's scapegoated subject C thus becomes the Kristevan abject or Agamben's *homo sacer*, the "unclean thing," via rhetoric, both visual and otherwise, existing at the opposite end of the spectrum from the sovereign, whose body is inviolable by any means (Agamben 84). A special state of exception is organized around that body, Agamben tells us, in which the rule of law may be suspended. It is important to note, though, that unlike Burke's sacrificial scapegoat, *homo sacer* is not the highest ideal contained within the lowest subject's sacrifice. Indeed, *homo sacer* has slipped so low that there are no "lower rungs," as Carter points out.

The greatest threat, then, to the individual is when the special case exception, which is a suspension of the law, becomes the law itself. Agamben reminds us that "when the state of exception . . . becomes the rule . . . then the juridico-political system becomes a machine which may at any moment turn lethal" (qtd. in de la Durantaye 337). This special case opens up a "no-man's land" between "civil law and political fact" at the site of the body of the scapegoated subject, the *homo sacer* (338). As Coats shows us, this is accomplished not just through rhetorical means but the very belief that the now-"unclean" subject must be expelled in horror by the lawful subject(s) in order to return balance to the social body. Subject C must be expelled. The only question that remains is whether subject C, the scapegoat, upon which the society may heap their failings and scorn and in exiling or killing, comes out cleansed or so low that they are no longer even sacrifice-able? The question is answered, as Agamben sees it, in that the state of exception may become the rule rather than the special cases: "The state of exception thus ceases to be referred to as an external and provisional state of factual danger and comes to be confused with juridical rule itself" (168; italics removed).

In some ways agreeing with Foucault, Agamben implies that there are underlying paradigms for life as we live it in relations to power. Whereas Foucault's paradigm is the panopticon, Agamben's is the concentration camp. "In the camp, the state of exception, which was essentially a temporary suspension of the rule of law on the basis of a factual state of danger, is now given a permanent spatial arrangement, which as such nevertheless remains outside the normal order" (169). His paradigm is not merely the panopticon of Foucault; it is the literal place, the concentration camp, where those contained within the boundaries are no longer sacred. They are no longer of value enough to sacrifice and may be tortured or even destroyed with little thought (de la Durantaye 213). "This will lead us to regard the camp not as a historical fact and an anomaly belonging to the past (even if still verifiable) but in some way as the hidden matrix ... of the political space in which we are still living" (Agamben 166). Agamben's metaphor may rankle when applied to our contemporary lives, but what if we were to propose the camp metaphor as an organizational strategy for the dystopian nations existing in young adult dystopian literature? As I will explore in chapter 3, this is a useful theoretical tool for examining the ways that these narratives expose interpellation in our own societies.

Lacanian Subject Formation

The Lacanian subject is formed via representation, beginning in the mirror stage. It is during that mirror stage, as Lacan theorizes it, that the child begins the process of exploring the distance between self and an idealized image of self. It is here that the child has "entered the world of signifying transactions, and image has displaced being" (Coats 19). In this way, language plays an enormous role in the formation of the subject, for language bridges this gap between the body and the idealized image.[3] Therefore, subjectivity is always a negotiated space of lack between the representational whole and the sense that there is something more. Coats says that "subjectivity, then, is more than identity ... it is a movement between that which we control and that which controls us" (5). It is in this way that we can understand the mirror stage as a kind of first instance of social formation, the point where language comes to form the foundation of subjectivity and is the instance that brings about the perception of the other.

Encountering the o/Other

There are many different ways to consider the nature of the term "the other" in various fields such as psychology, sociology, anthropology, linguistics, rhetoric, and literary criticism. Hélène Cixous has a particularly helpful explanation in the appendix of *The Newly Born Woman*. She says of the o/Other,

> in Lacanian theory, the ego is formed out of the internalization of the other. On another scale, whole cultures locate themselves in relation to things that they are not-their Other. Spelled with a lowercase "o," other is generally specifically experiential; with a capital "O," it is more hypothetical. Depending on one's situation, in its later manifestations, the Other can be what is repressed or the Law repressing it. (167)

In English studies, we tend toward two different conceptual models of the o/Other: the psychoanalytically inflected Lacanian perspective on the Other, and the more power-inflected other introduced into gender scholarship by Simone de Beauvoir. She shows that men have long considered themselves the default subject, with women forming the special case. Therefore all things stereotypically male have been thought of as "natural" or, worse, "normal," while all things stereotypically female are thought of as "other." The feminine becomes the devalued end of the gender binary; the other. She says,

> Now, what peculiarly signalizes the situation of woman is that she—a free and autonomous being like all human creatures—nevertheless finds herself living in a world where men compel her to assume the status of the Other. They propose to stabilize her as object and to doom her to

immanence since her transcendence is to be overshadowed and forever transcended by another ego. (xxxv)

In contrast, the Lacanian perspective posits the Other as that which is the not-I of the mirror self. Everything that is outside of the being that recognizes its bounded self in the image in the mirror takes on an "otherness" at that point.[4]

In contemporary English studies, while we often use both models, we tend to see the other as that space of devalued subjectivity in the binary ideological constructions that contemporary literature shows and/or reinforces. One of the ways we might begin to consider what this means is to follow gender and violence scholar Suzanne Hatty when she says, "The other may also be thought of as all that is alien, strange or different. The boundaries between self and other are often vigilantly policed so that the specter of mergence can be kept at bay" (11). In other words, self and other form the singular foundational binary that drives the formation of the subject. We can see this rigid policing of boundary in much of literature; however, I will later assert that it is science fiction that is unique as a literature for theorizing the contact between self and other in myriad ways rather than merely accepting such rejection of other as Hatty describes as a given.

Emmanuel Levinas believes that subjectivity comes into being through an encounter with another. Our ethical orientation toward that other is formed in that very instant of the encounter. In his foreword to de Certeau's *Heterologies*, Wlad Godzich attempts to summarize Levinas's concept of the pre-subjective encounter with the other:

> Levinas argues that there is a form of truth totally alien to me, that I do not discover within myself, but that calls on me from beyond me, and it requires me to leave the realms of the known and of the same in order to settle in a land that is under its rule. Here the knower sets out on an adventure of uncertain outcome, and the instruments that he or she brings may well be inappropriate to the tasks that will arise. Reason will play a role, but it will be a secondary one; it can only come into play once

the primary fact of the irruption of the other has been experienced ... in my originary encounter I discover my responsibility for the existence of this other, a responsibility that will lie at the root of all my subsequent ethical decision. Knowledge and its operations are subordinated to this initial ethical moment, for the responsibility that I then experience is the very ground of my response-ability, that is, my capacity to communicate with others and with myself in noncoercive ways. Reason can now deploy itself in the field that has been opened up by the relation I have to the other. (xvi)

Levinas believes that there is not subjectivity and then an encounter with another, but that the two things occur simultaneously. Alain Toumayan furthers our understanding by saying,[5]

> Since the subject is to be constituted by a relation to the other, and thus in a position of irreducible secondarity, subjectivity is a subjection ... a submission ... in this sense, the subject's condition can be compared to that of being held "hostage" by the other ... and something prior to consciousness or reason ... it also implies that in order to call himself present, the subject must be responding to the call of his responsibility for the other. (35)

Hence, a subject does not initially announce itself in the subjective, but does so first in the objective case. Difference, rather than constituting the place where subjectivity is in danger of breaking down, now becomes the encounter that is absolutely necessary for subjectivity to begin; "difference now serves to *define* the subject as a unity whose density and substantiality derive from a prior relation" (Toumayan 33). The most important part of Levinas's theory for us to use here is that the encounter with the other is essential for understanding subjectivity. Again, I believe that while dystopian literature takes the totalitarian abuse of power as its stock-in-trade, science fiction's focus is the encounter with the other—exposing the act of othering, itself, and the role it plays in subjectivity. While we may not pick up on Levinas's concern for ethics, his conception of subjectivity as born from the encounter with the other is something central to our examination of science fiction, especially when it is oriented toward the adolescent reader.

The Young Adult as Other

Adolescence is an othered subjectivity. The adolescent him or herself lives in a state of "otherness": abjected from the "cleanliness" of the social body and continually acted upon by the structures of power that surround him or her.

In explaining her thoughts on adolescent subjectivity, Karen Coats says,[6]

> at the level of the social, we think of adolescence in terms of the way it, like abjection, breaches and challenges boundaries. It is an in-between time, a time when what we know and believe about children is challenged, and where what we hope and value about maturity is challenged. Adolescents are both more and less sophisticated and knowing than we want them to be. They challenge the borders of identity, trying to become adult without becoming adulterated. Striving for social recognition but not wanting to stand out, locating with specificity their status as sexual subjects and objects, seeking the terms of individuation within affiliative groupings, adolescents are intensely involved in the construction of social boundaries and in reaffirming their distance from the socially abject. (142–43)

Coats sees this time in the life of the subject as a re-eruption of oedipal drama, as well as a time of rapid bodily change. The social conception of the child as pre-sexual is thrown into chaos as the newly emerging adolescent demonstrates undeniable movements toward sexuality. This creates a dilemma for the social body surrounding the young adult: eject the adolescent from the social order to preserve cleanliness, or accept the young adult into the order? It is at precisely that decision-making process that we can see the othered subjectivity of the adolescent—they exist on the edges of a web of power relations (and almost always occupy positions that have less power than the more accepted subjects such as adults).

Roberta Trites, also commenting on the adolescent as other, writes:

> Indeed, adolescents occupy an uncomfortable liminal space in America. Adolescents are both powerful (in the youthful looks and physical prowess that are glorified by Hollywood and Madison Avenue; in the increased economic power of the middle-class American teenagers as consumers; in the typical scenario of teenagers succeeding in their rebellions against authority figures) and disempowered (in the increased objectification of the teenage body that leads many adolescents to perpetrate acts of violence against the Self or Other; in the decreased economic usefulness of the teenager as a producer of goods in postindustrial America; in the typical scenario of teenagers rebelling against authority figures to escape oppression). (xi)

In order to conceive of the work that adolescent literature does, we must come to understand it as a socializing discourse (Trites 22–23). The literature earmarked for adolescent readers comes into the space that Coats theorizes, entering at the point where the social order has decided not to abject the subject, but instead to socialize it because "power is even more fundamental to adolescent literature than growth" (Trites x). If the subject wanders too far from the ISA cycle, he or she falls into the jurisdiction of the RSAs—starting first with the policing entities, then the judicial system, and finally to whatever form of incarceration the culture practices. The adolescent, in negotiating the extremely complex process of subjectivity at the hands of the ISAs, always has the choice to conform (which Foucault refers to as a Contract Oppression schema) or to rebel, thereby moving outside the ISAs and into the realm of the RSAs, where Foucault's Dominant-Oppression model takes over, and violence becomes socially viable for the state as a means to move the subject back toward the cycle of ISAs (Trites 3–7). Once more, the various discourses of power that shape our society, and the apparatuses in place to distribute those discourses, always have the adolescent under surveillance. These apparatuses are ready to apply corrective power in a continuum of force all the way from a casual verbal intervention through to violence. The adolescent is told quite clearly time and time again in adolescent literature that they have but one way to remain in the social order: make identificatory moves that clearly show interest in leaving the abject subject positions behind. Coats observes that "the abject characters thus act as foils and props for establishing the clean and proper identity of the normal protagonists, suggesting that one way out of abjection is the successful oedipalization of identity. Reciprocation into adult society requires leaving such figures behind" (151).

What might we say, then, about science fiction intended for a young adult audience as well as dystopian literature aimed at adolescents? In what ways do they participate in these power structures? What ontologies do they valorize, and which do they impose sanctions against?

Science Fiction for Young Adults

Young adult science fiction specifically helps the YA reader deconstruct the act of othering in their own subject formation. In this way, it is a genre intensely interested in demonstrating what we might call the Burkean end of the subject's interpellation. As critic Carl Freedman tells us, there are two major "tools" at work in science fiction: Darko Suvin's "cognitive estrangement" and Ernst Bloch's "novum." The first of these tools we must examine is Ernst Bloch's novum. Freedman tells us that the novum is that object or place that creates radical alterity, the "new thing" that immediately pulls readers out of their assumptions about how the world-within-the-fiction works and the realities of the author's empirical environment that the readers share. What we might think of as our normal ideological beliefs and rhetorical positions are estranged from us. With those rhetorical positions no longer available for the audience, they are in a position to see the issues in new ways.[7] That is the cognitive estrangement function as Suvin describes it: the contemporary situation in question may be examined more closely by removing the discourses that can often cloud the issue. A reader may then return to the contemporary discourses with new ideas. Most often this contemporary situation is one of othering, of encounters between devalued subjectivities. In other words, self and other form the singular foundational binary that drives the formation of the subject. Often, this is through a process that science fiction critics refer to as "coding." Metaphorically, the other of the narration stands in for some also-other in our empirical world. This encounter is meant as a mirror for some social relation already existing where significant othering has occurred. It is through this exploration of the coding of the other that the science fiction author can function as social critic.

I believe that it is important to note Jean Baudrillard's assertion that "from one order of simulacra to another, the tendency is certainly toward the reabsorption of the distance, of this gap that leaves room for an ideal or critical projection" (121–22). Science fiction, he says, can no longer be thought of as "unreal." In a postmodern world, where the map of the world is the same size and shape as the world, covering it, then science fiction is not merely critical of the "real world." It also maps and is mapped. As Adam Roberts reminds us, the narratives of spaceships are often far more fascinating to us than space missions carried out by flesh-and-blood astronauts (154). In other words, science fiction may sometimes *not* be used as a vehicle to gain distance on reality for critical endeavors, Baudrillard tells us. Still, as Žižek points out, we must not simply throw our hands up and reject the critical endeavor altogether. Science fiction can help us to problematize the process of othering as it occurs in the interplay between discourses and subjectivity.

The system of exploratory textual devices contained in the discourse of science fiction often attracts writers who have messages that would be unacceptable in more mainstream fiction. Feminist authors, for example, have become increasingly interested in science fiction as a means of exploring the limits of patriarchy and as a means of positing alternative social arrangements. As feminist critic Sarah Lefanu says, "The stock conventions of science fiction—time travel, alternate worlds, entropy, relativism, the search for a unified field theory—can be used metaphorically and metonymically as powerful ways of exploring the construction of 'woman'" (4–5). The feminist science fiction author can use the tools of science fiction to reach an audience that might not read a philosophy-only oriented text. Therefore, writing science fiction becomes important feminist consciousness-raising work.

I believe that there exist similar possibilities for children and young adults in science fiction, as well. Because of deeply entrenched ideology, the child is often constructed as the devalued end of our culture's experiential binary ("inexperienced"/"experienced"). Texts for them, we are so often told, are to be educational and entertaining, but not to allow them fully empowered subjectivity. Contemporary American ideology often demands that these texts are not to provide tools to enable transgression. Young adult science fiction, then, can be a place of some ideological turbulence, especially because of the tendency to see age/experience in such binary terms.

To examine how young adult science fiction works, then, we can put the theories of Trites into conversation with Freedman. He maintains that science fiction is inherently dialogic in its nature. This is due to the tension between cognition and estrangement (16). This tension creates in science fiction texts an inherent tendency to be *critical* texts, as well. Freedman believes that science fiction is always-already critically inclined, while Trites shows that in order to conceive of the work that adolescent literature does, we must come to understand it as a socializing discourse (22–23). Working closely with the theories of Althusser and showing the links to power and discourse theorist Foucault, she observes that surveillance and normalization are the forces at work in adolescent lit. In other words, the various discourses of power that shape our society and the apparatuses in place to distribute those discourses always have the adolescent under surveillance. This is the most important point to understanding the intersection between "young adult" and "science fiction": Trites believes that the vast majority of young adult texts are unaware of how they are functioning didactically as a discourse to suppress any radical subject positions in their readers, while Freedman believes that the science fiction text is inherently critical of such subject formation via discourse.

Dystopian Literature for Young Adults

Dystopian authors create texts that show the author functioning as cultural theorist in the subjunctive mode. Dystopian fiction is a genre where the author can readily engage contemporary social situations and theoretically project what is to come for an audience that is perhaps not always as theoretically or politically aware as an academic one. In essence, the genre is the logical extension of what is often called the slippery slope fallacy. Remember that Giorgio Agamben has said he believes that "today it is not the city, but rather the [concentration] camp that is the fundamental biopolitical paradigm of the West" (qtd. in de la Durantaye 213). Perhaps we might see, instead, that the dystopian society that mimics the concentration camp is the paradigm by which we can most clearly see Foucault's biopower being exercised. Hence, the dystopian literature narrative is the metaphor *par excellence* to demonstrate interpellation of the subject. Though the panopticon could be seen as the paradigm that functions within these dystopian narratives, in a sense, Agamben's paradigm of the concentration camp becomes the blueprint for the society of the narrative. The exceptional case of the suspension of law becomes the rule instead of the exception. It is in this extremist example of how a society functions that the adolescent can begin to see more clearly the webs of force and subjectivity that may be more obscured in the world outside the narrative that they occupy. Fredric Jameson says, "the best Utopias can serve the negative purpose of making us more aware of our mental and ideological imprisonment ... and that therefore the best Utopias are those that fail the most comprehensively" (xiii). I would disagree and say that they point out our subjectivity in its totality, and that this is not imprisonment.

Often, when reading one of these works, we are left with a sense of unease about the future. I suggested earlier that Burkean identification, through the social lens of the work of Althusser and Foucault, is the primary way in which the state monitors normative ideological formation of the subject in these fictions, creating whole herds of Agamben's *homo sacer*. Dystopian works attempt to make this system transparent. These authors are functioning as cultural theorists showing the worst-case scenario of how the state first confines (Foucauldian surveillance) and then defines (Althusserian structures) the citizen as one that has had its (Žižekian) pre-ideological kernel bent toward accepting the suspension of its (Agambenian) sense of self-as-more-than-cattle via rhetorical structures (Burkean identification). When examining this genre we are left with a series of texts that not only show the various tactics and rhetorics the state might employ to force identification with officially sanctioned figures, but also how this same strategy is used to create figures that the subject is supposed to scapegoat.

Childhood itself is often theorized as a utopia that exists until adult intervention (Sands and Frank 78). This conservative, pastoral-driven, romantic impulse is present in the dystopian narrative. Through the power of repressive strategies, the regime within the narrative often tries to recreate the citizen subject of their society as childlike. In essence, the state is often engaged in infantilizing its entire population. The infantilized state of the populace is produced by the strict codes and mores, and this uncomplicated state is often seen as utopia by readers. Sands and Frank remind us, though, that there is little hope for the subject to change or gain agency within that system. The "lack of hope" they describe in the text, however, actually stands in to give the reader hope. As Bullen and Parsons say of such narratives, "In this way, the act of reading becomes the impetus to action" (38). The point of such a narrative is to inspire the reader to action. This is accomplished through the urge to dis-identify, in a Burkean sense, with the type of regime depicted in the text. "We need to pass through the critical dystopias of today to move toward a horizon of hope" (Baccolini 521). In reaching for that horizon, the focalizer, so long infantilized by the repressive regime, moves into adolescence—a breaking away from childhood into self-reliance and responsibility.

Dystopian texts intended for children and young adults show a metaphorization of the movement from childhood to adolescence. Trites's view of young adult fiction is that the genre functions most often as "a discourse of institutional socialization" for the adolescent (22). More often than not, the YA novel seeks to reassert the state's dominance over the individual through both repression and formation via surveillance. She further reminds us that, while some characters seem to gain power within the structure of the novel, in the end it is most often the state that gains control by normalizing the adolescent character via the narrative. These texts show the various power discourses at work on the adolescent as he or she moves from metaphoric childhood "utopia" to metaphoric adolescent "dystopia." I take very seriously Trites's assertion that the YA text itself forms a part of the web of controls, in other words, and that any definition of growth for a character (or, indeed, for a reader) can only be accomplished within the bounds of institutions—any "escape" from one institution's power leading only to the grasp of another institution. Transcendence, she points out, meaning a move outside of the influence of any institutional power, is not possible and not a definition of growth that we can use in relationship to these texts (Trites 17–18). "[E]verything in culture is constituted by discourse and all discourse participates in the modes of production that enact society, then nothing escapes the capitalist institution. We are all subjects constituted by discourse, so we are all immersed irrevocably in capitalism" (Trites 17–18). The YA dystopian text is caught in this very bind—like all YA novels, the protagonist is shown maturing in their conception of their relationships to the various discourses controlled by the institutions of their particular society, but it must also show that protagonist escaping the repressive regime or else the reader is likely to consider the book not very satisfying. The tricky move the author must create is to show that the protagonist moves from the institutions of the repressive state into another set of institutions that feel to the protagonist and hopefully the audience to be a less repressive state and to make this move look like freedom has been achieved. The usefulness of this genre is that it shows more clearly the ways that societies construct the subject (in this case, the child or adolescent); it makes the often-invisible formative discourses visible by metaphor.

The Use Value of Genre

It is important for us to understand these genres, then, so that we might deploy them in ways that help adolescent readers. Rather than use the study of genre as a form of hierarchy, we might view the question of genre as a way of talking about texts and their relationships to readers. David Duff believes that "the word genre now seems to have lost most of its negative charge and to be operating instead as a valorising term, signaling not prescription and exclusion but opportunity and common purpose" (2).

Perry Nodelman, in his book *The Pleasure of Children's Literature*, does this type of work by examining genre not for the purpose of prescription, but instead to outline the relationship between the genres and their readers, ideologically. These "implied readers" have expectations, normative pressures, developmental levels, and a variety of reading needs. In other words, genre examination works best not as some prescriptive force of judgment, but as an examination of relationship between reader, text, and culture. This is what I also intend when I use the term *genre* here. Thomas O. Beebee tells us that most genre criticism to date has come in one of four stages. He says that "these four stages of generic criticism—genre as rules, genre as species, genre as patterns of textual feature, and genre as reader conventions—correspond to the four positions in the great debate about the location of textual meaning: in authorial intention, in the work's historical and literary context, in the text itself, or in the reader" (3). Here, I intend none of those approaches to genre. Instead, I intend to use Beebee's own orientation, an orientation toward genre as *use value*. He writes, "I began to see genre as a set of 'handles' on texts, and to realize that a text's genre is its use value. Genre gives us not understanding in the abstract and passive sense but *use* in the pragmatic and active sense" (14; emphasis mine). It is essential that we recognize that "not only literary but also extra-literary systems—political, social, religious and so on—contribute significantly to the shape of literary forms" (Dubrow 112). Cultural attitudes shape genre forms, and the reverse also happens. Heather Dubrow reminds us, "Moreover, much like a firmly rooted institution, a well-established genre transmits certain cultural attitudes, attitudes which it is shaped by and in turn helps to shape" (4). Todorov showed that "like any other institution, genres bring to light the constitutive features of the society to which they belong" (200). In this way, we can see that genre is both *shaped by* ideology at the same time that it *shapes* ideology. As both Beebee and Dubrow point out, genre does a particular kind of work on the reader. Indeed, some twenty years before Beebee, Tzvetan Todorov had already been working with the assumption that genre was more about relations of discourses to text than about some bound set of rules for separating the "good" from the "bad" works. He said,

> Genres are thus entities that can be described from two different viewpoints, that of empirical observation and that of abstract analysis. In a given society, the recurrence of certain discursive properties is

institutionalized, and individual texts are produced and perceived in relation to the norm constituted by that codification. A genre, whether literary or not, is nothing other than the codification of discursive properties. (198)

This is precisely where I wish to start the conversation about genre: with the realization that each genre does a particular kind of work on the reader, just as it is worked on by the society. The sense of a genre's use value comes from exploring those relationships. In the case of this inquiry, we are examining the use values of science fiction for adolescents and dystopian literature for young adults. What is it that they are doing, and how might we, through a better understanding of what they are doing, use them?

The first point we must address is that science fiction and dystopian literature are often thought of as existing one within the border of the other. There is a sense that these genres do the same work and so may be classified as the same, but this is not actually the case, as I will demonstrate below. An examination of the boundaries of these genres will give us a better sense of the work that they are doing. Indeed, as Beebee says, "not only are genre systems ideological, but their cusps provide a most advantageous place from which to observe workings of ideology in literature" (17). It is these very cusps, this very contact zone of interaction between adolescent science fiction and dystopian literature for young adults that I wish to examine. I believe this conversation about genre to be a necessary one. My goal is to examine the relationship between science fiction and dystopian literature as a way of separating out their use values to us as critics, instructors, and librarians in the pursuit of helping young people to better see their subjectivity in relation to the discourses around them.

2

"The Electric Boy[1] Grows Up": Science Fiction for a Young Adult Audience

> *Science fiction, which has conventionally used the future to comment on the present and the alien to comment on the familiar, provides an ideal site from which to explore the liminal, the brink, the verge, the frontier, the edge ... More and more writers are turning to science fiction as a narrative discourse through which to map the metamorphoses of present reality.*
> —Gordon and Hollinger, 4

Science fiction can be used to help adolescents examine the "us/them" orientation of the discourse that surrounds them. The genre does so by examining the encounter with the other.[2] Science fiction critic Martha Bartter says, "while SF has frequently been termed an 'escapist' literature, it has often been the forum for the most thoughtful and serious considerations of humanity's most worrisome problems" (136). Science fiction accomplishes these considerations by allowing the readers to experience a "radical alterity," as critic Adam Roberts calls it. Darren Harris-Fain says "science fiction is a literature of change—radical, evolutionary change. A key facet of dealing with such change, many critics would argue, is the fact that SF writers are able to both posit radical changes in their stories and extrapolate the possibilities that might result" (5–6).

Young adult science fiction specifically helps YA readers deconstruct the act of othering in their own subject formation by posing radical change: within these texts, the author can show the encounter with the other, and possible results. In this way, it is a genre intensely interested in demonstrating what we might call the Burkean end of the subject's interpellation. Adolescents are very busy assembling and synthesizing concurrent ideological strands within their contemporary culture. If we can divorce an issue from those nodal points, then what we can provide them is some "equipment for living," as Burke would have it.[3] Children's literature critic C. W. Sullivan III tells us that we should use children's and YA SF texts in order to "prepare readers for the future by exposing them to a variety of possible futures ... giving them some fictional experience in dealing with the new, the unusual, and *the challenging*" (3; emphasis mine). Science fiction for young adults is, in a sense, a genre of thought experiment designed to bring the adolescent to the encounter with the other.

It is important to note, here, that in this chapter I am not talking about the broader term "speculative fiction." This term tends to include sword-and-sorcery fantasy. I differentiate science fiction from speculative fiction in the same way that Fredric Jameson does; by noting the difference between science fiction and fantasy.[4] He says that he believes that there are two main structural characteristics that form the foundational difference between science fiction and fantasy, "the ethical binary of good and evil, and the fundamental role it assigns to magic" (58). In chapter 5 of *Archaeologies of the Future*, Jameson shows that he feels the differences between science fiction and fantasy come down to this: Fantasy is about ethics, and about faith, while science fiction is about politics and science. Of course, when he says this, he means the ethics that are involved in the particular manifestations of technology and scientific discovery, so the boundary between the two is tenuous. I recognize this. Once again, though, I make these distinctions because of use value. I believe that we must begin to differentiate between these genres, not by defaulting to some hierarchy of artistic legitimacy, but instead by examining their use values, if we wish to use them responsibly in classrooms and libraries.

The History of the Future

Francis J. Molson suggests that science fiction emerged as a genre from the Industrial Revolution, especially the SF intended for a young audience. He believes that it was the orientation of youth at the time toward the advancements in technology that made them hungry for narratives filled with even more creative advancements. Isaac Asimov, one of the distinguished few SF writers who are both scientists and writers, would later say of SF:

> We can then define science fiction as that branch of literature that deals with the human response to changes in the level of science and technology—it being understood that the changes involved would be rational ones in keeping with what we know about science, technology and people. True science fiction, by its modern definition (or at least, *my* modern definition) could not have been written prior to the nineteenth century then, because it was only with the coming of the Industrial Revolution in the last few decades of the eighteenth century that the rate of technological change became great enough to notice in a single lifetime—in those areas of the globe affected by that revolution. (11)

However, while he, like most critics, attributes the rise of the scientific romance almost solely to the Industrial Revolution, there were other factors at work. Primary among those was the shift in how the sciences were viewed, as well as the rigid structuring of the British publication system of the day.[5]

Suzanne Elizabeth Reid cites Lester del Rey's conception of "Five Ages of Science Fiction" as a useful way of understanding how the genre evolved from the mid-1920s to the early 1980s (11). She paraphrases del Rey by stating that the first age was what he called "The Age of Wonder," which he says lasted from 1926 through 1937. During this time, science fiction was predominantly distributed by pulp magazines. His second age was "The Golden Age" from 1938 through 1949. Though still predominantly a pulp magazine era, this is the age that saw the beginnings of the careers of Asimov and Heinlein. Though not the "fathers" of the field, these are two authors whose works del Rey and others feel elevate the genre to its highest form.[6] The third age del Rey refers to was "The Age of Acceptance," from 1950 to 1961, when the paperback novel begins to replace the pulp magazine as the primary mode for science fiction distribution. It is during this period, too, that the science fiction film becomes common, with such classics as *Invasion of the Body Snatchers* and *Forbidden Planet* both released in 1956. It is during this time that the conception of science fiction as the genre for the young also takes hold. The fourth age that del Ray proposes was "The Age of Rebellion," which runs from 1962 through 1973. There is new sophistication in the writing style of many new authors introduced through anthologies, published for the first time during this period. Science fiction becomes much more the staple of television and film than print during this period of time. This is the heyday of the original run of *Star Trek* on television, and *Planet of the Apes* and all four of its sequel films fall squarely in this period. The fifth age he proposes doesn't have a particular name as he saw it, and runs from 1974 through the present (which, at the time he published, was 1980). This is the period of a particularly nihilistic strain of science fiction, which del Rey publishes too early to note, called cyberpunk, that combines the aesthetics and societal-underbelly-centeredness of Noir film with questions of ontology in the face of the human/machine hybridization called cybernetics (Reid 11–13).[7]

It is somewhat unfortunate that del Rey was not also charting the history of science fiction intended for young people in his ages. Francis J. Molson shows that there is quite a bit of what he calls "young inventor fiction" occurring before the 1920s that del Rey thinks of as the first age. Molson, as well as Karen Sands and Marietta Frank, point specifically to the Stratemeyer Syndicate's Tom Swift series, published between 1910 and 1941 (7). They go on to say: "However, with the decline of the Tom Swift series in the late 1930s and the shortages of World War II, juvenile readers had few new titles from which to select. The science fiction available to juveniles between 1939 and 1945 amounted to science fiction comics, a few juvenile novels, and adult pulp science fiction" (1–2). The post-WWII era, though, saw an explosion of science fiction for young people, most notably the revival of Tom Swift in the Tom Swift Jr. series: "The themes moved beyond 'gee whiz' attitude toward technology" (2). Sands and Frank go on to say,

> While Earth might have to endure overpopulation, resource shortages, and pollution, humans could colonize other planets, or even the ocean's bottom, to offer humankind a second chance. Hiroshima showed the more sinister side of scientific and technological applications, but in the world of the juvenile science fiction series, science and technology still proffered some hope for humanity. (2)

As post–WWII America became aware that there was a category of existence called "teenager," literature that addressed their specific concerns grew. During this period, science fiction was primarily concerned with fulfillment of fantasies such as the desire for power, for approval from those with power, or simply to get the girl, so to speak. Jānis Svilpis says:

> Through most of its history, then, science fiction, even ostensibly adult pulp science fiction, has been geared to children's concerns. Perhaps it might be more accurate to say childish concerns, since much of it

consists of unreflective and vacuous wish-fulfillment. The appeal of Burroughs, Smith, and many of their fellows was based on fast action, violence of sometimes cosmic proportions, a sexuality so thoroughly sublimated that talking to a woman was like establishing contact with an alien being, and a sense of intellectual and moral security firmly founded on unexamined assumptions. Not all magazine science fiction was flawed in these ways, but much of what was worst in it influenced the science fiction for adolescents that became a separate category after the Second World War. (26)

Heinlein's *Rocket Ship Gallileo*, the beginning of what is referred to as his "Heinlein Juveniles" series, was published in 1947. Asimov's *David Starr, Space Ranger*, the beginning of his "Lucky Starr" series, was published in 1952. Both were intended for young readers of science fiction, and seem to follow the patterns of young adults swept up into larger matters such as galactic wars and providing the needed solution to them.

The more sociological turn that del Rey describes, though, occurs in juvenile science fiction as well. Madeleine L'Engle's *A Wrinkle in Time* is published in 1962 and demonstrates the turn from technology and exploration to social problem solving. By the seventies, science fiction had taken what Roberts and others call an introspective turn. Though the technological component was still important, the stories in both "adult" and YA science fiction began to explore conditions of existence. Currently, I believe that we are in what many call a post-cyberpunk or post-human moment, where the characters experiencing the impact of technology on their very definitions of being-ness are no longer fringe elements such as hackers or others who work on the black market, but adults and teens living what we might call "suburban" existences.[8]

In short, as early as 1962, science fiction for young people no longer relied as heavily on an orientation toward technology as its primary motivation; the history of the genre must lead us to see that it is a discourse focused on asking critical questions. Merely setting a story in the future or filling a story with technological gadgets does not make it science fiction—the critical questioning must be present.[9] If this is the case, then we are left with the question, how does this genre perform the work of such interrogation?

A Grammar of Science Fiction

Science fiction is a discourse that allows us to examine our own world through the lens of metaphor, so it is a genre that lends itself to critically examining culture. SF does this particularly well because of a set of tools inherent to the genre. Mendlesohn has said she believes that there is a "grammar of science fiction" and that science fiction is less of a genre than a mode, a way of writing things (287). Adam Roberts would agree, I think; he points out that science fiction is a way of exploring the metaphoric within a realist mode of prose. However, Mendlesohn goes on to say that technology and a sense of wonder are the main points of science fiction:

> When the novel comes to privilege the personal over the political, scientific or social, to see the science fictional plot as an external space in which to work out strategies to apply to one's beginning point (usually home life), rather than to lead one out into the universe, it frequently loses those qualities that are associated with SF. The SF adventure becomes metaphor; it does not matter in and of itself, but is subordinate to the *bildungsroman* of family or school crisis. The effect is to diminish the sense of wonder intrinsic to SF. (291–92)

I disagree; the technology and the "sense of wonder" may have been the point of the scientific romance of the nineteenth century (and some of that remains in strains of "hard" science fiction), but contemporary science fiction is engaged with the encounter with the other and exploring the nature of the act of othering itself. While I agree with Farah Mendlesohn's point that the science-fiction-ness of

YA SF may sometimes be in question, I think that if we conceive of science fiction's purpose as being the very inward-turn that she feels ruins the technological forward-looking-ness of the genre, then we see that the genre is doing some important work. The metaphoric examination of the contemporary social setting within the YA SF novel is not an interruption to science fiction, but is, rather, its point.

Mendlesohn's assertion that there is a grammar of science fiction is accurate, however. As I discussed in chapter 1, critic Carl Freedman tells us, there are two major "tools" at work in science fiction: Darko Suvin's "cognitive estrangement" and Ernst Bloch's "Novum." Freedman quotes Suvin as saying that science fiction is "a literary genre whose necessary and sufficient conditions are the presence and interaction of estrangement and cognition and whose main formal device is an imaginative framework alternative to the author's empirical environment" (16). The first of these tools is Ernst Bloch's novum. Freedman tells us that the novum is that object or place that creates radical alterity; that is, it is the "new thing" that immediately pulls the reader out of their assumptions about the similarity between the way the world-within-the-fiction works to the "author's empirical environment." The novum pulls us out of our assumptions of how narrative normally progresses. In this way, the novum is the impetus for the dialogic nature of science fiction.[10] The Blochian novum is the "new thing" that radically alters our perception of the realist-based prose of the rest of the novel enough to gain cognitive estrangement. The intervention of the novum into the narrative defamiliarizes us from the familiar trajectories we might expect of the narrative at hand. In this way, we become cognitively estranged. We can now see the embedded social relations that often seem too complex to fathom in our empirical world through a new lens. It is the encounter with the novum that pulls readers out of their traditional expectations of how the narrative will progress. At that moment, a dialogic relationship begins between reader and text—a space is opened up for skepticism and inquiry rather than just acceptance of the narrative. This is cognitive estrangement.

The process of cognitive estrangement allows the science fiction author to examine a contemporary issue by stripping away some of those contemporary world discourses. What we might think of as our normal ideological beliefs and rhetorical positions are estranged from us. With those rhetorical positions no longer available for the audience, they are in a position to see the issue in new ways.[11] This is by no means an attempt to suggest that any issue is simple. Instead, I mean to say that the situation in question may be examined more closely by removing the discourses that can often cloud the issue. A reader may then return to the contemporary discourses with new ideas.

A good example of this is in Ned Vizzini's novel *Be More Chill*. In the novel, Jeremy, an outcast, is continually nursing the wound of his somewhat self-imposed outsider subject position.[12] Through rumor and an odd interaction with one of his bullies, he hears about a pill-form supercomputer called a Squib. With that Squib's amazing abilities and advice, Jeremy gains power within the school structure, coming to see the power structures and lines of othering in high school to be coping mechanisms of others who are just as insecure and hurting as he is.

As we read part 1 of the novel, we become fully immersed in the narrative of an awkward high school boy. The idea of a super miniaturized computer that you swallow and suddenly become amazing seems like a wild goose chase; the realist approach of the prose leads us to believe that we are dealing with a world in which there could not be such an object. And then, suddenly, in part 2 of the novel, Jeremy finds someone who has a Squib, and is willing to sell it to him. We are expecting this to be a lesson on gullibility and for Jeremy to learn an important lesson about himself here. Instead, we are quite surprised when, after swallowing the pill, it works,

TING.
Whoa. Here we go.
WELCOME TO SQUIP 2.5.

> It's my voice, in my head, but it isn't all that strange. It's like my own voice, but deeper, older, more authoritative. It sounds like—
>
> "Keanu Reeves?"
>
> "Yeah! You're hearing it?" Rack stands up.
>
> "It's *Keanu Reeves's voice*?"
>
> "Sure, but that's just the default." (104)[13]

Suddenly, we are yanked out of our perception that this might be a typical school story about a lonely kid who chases after coolness only to find he had it all along. In its place, we are left with something new—the boy really *has* ingested a supercomputer. The reaction of the second character makes us sure that we cannot merely dismiss the occurrence as mental illness—Rack knows what Jeremy is hearing, and confirms for both Jeremy and for us as an audience that this is part of the technology. Because of this intervention, we are no longer able to view the high school experience that Jeremy has from this point forward in the narrative from our embedded conceptions of how high school works. Instead, we are now viewing high school both through the experience of a boy trapped within it, so to speak, as well as a computer that is outside of it. This dialectic point of view of the narrative allows us as readers to interrogate Jeremy's experiences critically.

This also happens in Walter Mosely's 2005 novel, *47*. For the first sixty-five pages of the novel, we are immersed in what we might call a fairly standard pre–Civil War slave narrative. The historical realist mode has had just enough time to set in, when we hit the novum: Tall John's sleep machine:

> Upon saying these words John reached into his pocket and came out with a metal tube that looked something like a tin cigar. There were red and green and blue beads up and down the sides of the tube that shone almost as if there was a tiny candle behind each one. On the top was a black button like a brimless hat.
>
> "Did you hear a tiny chime?" he asked me.

"I sho did."
"That was my little sleep machine here." (65)

Immediately, we as readers from a gadget-oriented culture recognize that this is some sort of device. Seeing a device of this sort after having just enough time to convince ourselves that we would see nothing more technologically advanced than a locomotive or riverboat instantly pulls us as readers out of our assumptions of how the story will unfold.

It is because of this interruption of the expected trajectory of the narrative that we come to accept John's behavior as something more than merely mental instability. After all, there is always the chance that John is crazy. However, once the novum happens, when 47 asks about John's home, he says,

> "My home," he said, "is very different from anything in Georgia or anywhere else on Earth. It has red skies and floating lakes and many of the animals can speak and use tools."
> "Horses that can swing a hammah?" I asked.
> "Like that," he said in the dark, "yes."
> "That's crazy talk." (73)

And, indeed, it seems to be. After encountering so much historical realism, this seems fanciful. As readers, we think about the strange behavior John has exhibited, and we begin to think that perhaps John has lost his mind. When 47 asks him if he has ever been home since arriving, John says, "Only in my mind" (73). Now that we have experienced the textual intervention of the novum, though, we are left with an uncertainty—maybe he really is an alien being. This helps us to see the institution of slavery from the outside because we are no longer embedded in the subjective experience of a character who thinks within the confines of the ideological constructs of the time period; we cannot dismiss John's opinions on slavery as perhaps the talk of a seemingly crazy person anymore, nor is the reader left merely with their own. Instead, we are left in dialogic tension: from this space we can critically examine the narrative of slavery.

A Literature of Critical Advocacy

The system of exploratory textual devices contained in the discourse of science fiction often attracts writers who have messages that would be unacceptable in more mainstream fiction. Feminist authors, for example, have become increasingly interested in science fiction as a means of exploring the limits of patriarchy and as a means of positing alternative social arrangements. As feminist SF critic Sarah Lefanu says, "The stock conventions of science fiction—time travel, alternate worlds, entropy, relativism, the search for a unified field theory—can be used metaphorically and metonymically as powerful ways of exploring the construction of 'woman'" (4–5). The feminist science fiction author can use the tools of science fiction to reach an audience that might not read a philosophy-only oriented text. Therefore, writing science fiction becomes important work for feminist consciousness-raising. In fact, we might think of feminist science fiction as having an advocacy trajectory.

In the editor's foreword of *The Feminine Eye*, critic Tom Staicar says that he believes one of the reasons feminist critics and writers are so drawn to the SF genre is that there are possibilities for exploring ideas forbidden to more "mainstream" fiction. He says,

> Science fiction has lured a number of new writers from the feminist movement partly because only SF permits unlimited freedom in settings . . . Mainstream novels restrict their writers either to a historical setting where sex roles are already established, or to contemporary settings where potential future sex roles do not exist except for isolated individuals. Only science fiction allows the freedom to create a "laboratory" world where one can experiment. (vii)

As a result of the increase of female and feminist SF authors, most texts produced during the New Wave (science fiction of the '70s) and after tend to cognitively estrange gender role ideology, positing alternative ways of seeing the seemingly binary situation. Writers who do make the effort to break out of such a sterile, laboratory pattern are often writing texts that explore the presence and inherent untidiness of the body and its drives.

For example, Sarah Lefanu reminds us that

> A useful way to begin might be to see what science fiction *allows* . . . By borrowing from other literary forms it lets writers defamiliarize the familiar, and make familiar the new and strange. These twin possibilities, apparently contradictory (but SF is full of contradictions), offer enormous scope to women writers who are thus released from the constraints of realism. The social and sexual hierarchies of the contemporary world can be examined through the process of "estrangement," thus challenging normative ideas of gender roles; and visions of different worlds can be created, made familiar to the reader through the process of narrative. SF narrative can be used to break down, or to build. (21–22)

The feminist science fiction author can use the tools of science fiction to reach an audience that might not read a philosophy-only oriented text. In this way, he or she can create a textual intervention between the subject who is reading and gender normative ideology.

Also a Literature of Critical Advocacy

Much like feminist science fiction, I believe that science fiction for young adults also has an advocacy angle because the inherent dialogic, critical nature of the genre automatically calls into question ideological construction/pressures faced by young adults. Farah Mendlesohn writes,

> Part of my argument is that this depends less on the images and contextual markers of SF than it does on a way of thinking about the world which requires authors to offer a type of challenge which moves away from an assumption that literature for children should reinforce what they already recognize. (286)

Science fiction's properties make it a genre that asks the reader to look closely at the society that is constructing him or her. As Coats asserts, the adolescent is under strong pressure to conform or be expelled from the social body. And as Trites asserts, literature for adolescents is an enormous force for socialization. Thus, ontological possibility is sanctioned by the narratives adolescents consume. A critically aware YA SF writer, then, has the possibility of creating a text that intervenes in the normative ideological constructions by calling into question the assumption that they are "natural." As I discussed in chapter 1, putting theories of how adolescent literature socializes adolescents into conversation with Carl Freedman helps in the examination of how young adult science fiction works.

Freedman maintains that science fiction is inherently dialogic in its nature. This is due to the tension between cognition and estrangement (16). This tension creates in science fiction texts an inherent tendency to be *critical* texts, as well. Freedman believes that science fiction is always-already critically inclined. Science fiction, he tells us, "maintains a cutting edge of social subversion even at its most rarefied and abstract" (8). So, what we might expect, given Freedman's theory, is that the science fiction text is a work that is designed to question the dominant structure of contemporary society, a genre of hegemonic resistance. He maintains that, through the tendencies of science fiction discourse, such as the novum, the reader is allowed to move into a place of meta-cognition, able to see the discourses moving around and shaping the subject-protagonist.[14] By extension, readers might then gain some insight into their own position as subject to these same discourses.

Trites's text, *Disturbing the Universe*, shows that in order to conceive of the work that adolescent literature does, we must come to understand it as a socializing discourse (22–23). Working closely with the theories of Althusser and showing the links to power and discourse that Foucault postulates, Trites observes that surveillance and normalization are dominant forces at work in adolescent literature. In other words, the various discourses of power that shape our society and the apparatuses in place to distribute those discourses always have the adolescent under surveillance. Trites states that the young adult fiction functions most often as "a discourse of institutional socialization" for the adolescent (22). More often than not, the YA novel seeks to reassert the state's dominance over the individual through both repression and formation via surveillance. She further reminds us that, while some characters seem to gain power within the structure of the novel, in the end, it is most often the state which gains control by normalizing the adolescent character via the narrative.

This is the most important point to understanding the intersection between "young adult" and "science fiction"; Trites believes that the vast majority of young adult texts are unaware of how they are functioning didactically as a discourse to suppress any radical subject positions in their readers, while Freedman believes that the science fiction text is inherently critical of such subject formation via discourse. This is a spot of tension between the two: Freedman believes that science fiction is always-already critically inclined, while Trites's text holds between its lines a call to authors to make their works more critical of power and the apparatuses that maintain it.

In the case of science fiction for adolescents, more often than not the author moves for reabsorption of the critical element, as I will demonstrate when we discuss *I Was a Teenage Popsicle*. This is why science fiction for young people often falls short of being artistically satisfying: the endings seem marred by the move back to status quo after a space of radical possibility has been opened. Regardless, that space is opened at some point within the text, and this is why the genre becomes important. I am not advocating that we ignore the endings of all these novels; however, we cannot ignore that the machinery of science fiction produces radical alterity and that possibility exists in those spaces. I believe that there exist liberatory possibilities for children and young adults in science fiction. Because of deeply entrenched ideology, the child is often constructed as the devalued end of our culture's experiential spectrum. Texts for them, we are so often told, are to be educational and entertaining, but not to allow them transgressive tools. Our contemporary American ideology often demands that these texts are not to provide tools to enable transgression. Young adult science fiction, then, can be a place of some ideological turbulence, with authors struggling at times to move the powerful current of critical awareness present in the science fiction text back to a status quo. We should not ignore, though, that within that turbulence, too, can be a space of possibility and critical reflection.

Defamiliarizing the Familiar

It is in this way that the familiar is defamiliarized enough, is cognitively estranged enough, for us to see it anew. Sands and Frank theorize that this is one of the essential differences, though, between science fiction intended for children and that intended for young adults. They say, "Whereas children's science fiction series attempt in various ways to make the unknowable known, young adult science fiction series—despite retaining familiarity through constant characters—make the familiar into something strange and unknown" (28). I would press that further by saying that this binary relationship of estrangement to text is not merely a condition of serialized fiction for young audiences, but is in fact a generalized genre characteristic. The work that the novum/cognitive estrangement pairing does in these situations differs: for children, Sands and Frank say, the idea is to make the child comfortable with the unknown. We see this manifested in such things as a family trip into space, or a robot who acts like a little boy.[15] For young adults, however, the object is to make the reader unfamiliar enough with things that are commonplace as a way to see them anew. We see this manifested in such tropes as the teacher who turns out to be an alien.[16] "[T]hus, series science fiction for children, despite its often alien settings or characters, contains a considerable amount of recognizable and/or comforting material for the young audience" (Sands and Frank 23), and in science fiction intended for young adults we see much less material designed to comfort the reader.

A large component of cognitive estrangement is coding. In science fiction criticism, the metaphoric relationships of estrangement (i.e., teacher as alien, etc.) are referred to as "coding" by Adam Roberts (and others). Science fiction's primary relationship with the world it reflects is through this mechanism of coding. The other then does not simply signify "otherness" but instead stands in for some relationship in the world outside the text, the reader's empirical environment. This encounter is meant as a mirror for some social relation already existing where significant othering has occurred. For instance, texts that involve an exploration of the relationships between humans and robots have long been understood to code for an exploration of slavery in America and its lasting aftereffects on race relations.[17] By discussing the robot and its status as devalued other in the culture of the narrative, the science fiction author can show ideologies at work in a way that will perhaps make an impact on readers who might not have listened, or had access to critical texts, before. Through coding the other, science fiction author can function as social critic. Roberts says,

> In the science fiction aliens, his unadmitted sense of the mysteriousness of others is given the objective correlative, as Grierson and Eliot called it, for feelings that are always inside him. He is in the process of shifting from a world centered upon him to one in which he is just an individual in a crowd of people whose inbuilt purposes are taking them in other

directions. He will come to accept this more easily, I suspect, when the otherness is given an unmistakably alien form. (89–90)

With the Other safely coded, the reader is much more likely to accept the dialogic interrogation of ideology and identification as explained in chapter 1. This is not to say that the coded Other is not transgressive in many ways. In fact, as Gordon says,

> In novels of alien contact, as in the history of colonization, the first impulse of human confrontation with the alien, the Other, is to annihilate it. This annihilation may occur through familiarization: by assimilating or by "passing," by absorbing or being absorbed by the dominant culture. That is the peaceful method. Or the annihilation may occur through erasure: by expulsion or killing. (205)

In these ways we can see that othering is not simply the act of posing an "I" or a "we" in opposition to a "they" (A not equaling C in the Burkean terms explored earlier), but also in the actions/reactions of the characters to that other. As I described in chapter 1, the other is essential to subject formation—so essential that Hatty says that the subject may only be posed by being opposed. The coded other, and the move of othering, then, enter the dialogue between text and reader as a way of exposing ideological relationships. The reactions of the characters are meant to demonstrate to the reader possibilities that exist in relationship to whatever it is the particular coded other in question stands in for.

The Family in Disguise

In contemporary science fiction for adolescents, it seems to me that the relationship in the empirical world that is most often estranged for examination is that of the child to the family. Mendlesohn says she feels, "Where SF for adults frequently deploys protagonists without family, and has long been considered the fiction of those who eschew the idea that literature is about inter-personal relationships, modern SF for children and young adults frequently uses the family as either context or motivation" (285). Elaine Ostry agrees in many ways, saying that she feels, "like the definition of 'human' itself, the family structure in the posthuman age must accommodate the advances of science" (234). While I am somewhat unconvinced that we live in something called the "posthuman age," I take Ostry's point (like Harraway's *cyborg* concept before her) that we are at a level currently where technology affects ontology in profound ways. And as our culture changes, and the nuclear family becomes less a model for how families are formed and function, science fiction for young people begins to examine the shifting patterns of kinship. Science fiction's cognitive estrangement allows us to interrogate these changes.

An example of this occurs in Bev Katz Rosenbaum's 2006 novel, *I Was a Teenage Popsicle*. In the novel, we meet Floe Ryan, who was sixteen when she contracted lympaticotosis (a fictional respiratory disease that we are told is fatal and incurable by the standards of the time). In hopes that eventually it might be curable, though, Floe (along with others) is vitrified and awakens ten years in the future.[18] This is a wonderful reversal in many ways, because most of the texts that feature what we might somewhat playfully call "the Rip Van Winkle trope" focus in on a *male* protagonist who awakens hundreds of years in the future.[19] Not only is there a gender reversal involved, but Rosenbaum uses the device to focus in on Floe's journey as adolescent rather than as a way to explore a utopic setting.[20] Rosenbaum's use of this trope is meant to allow us to defamiliarize family relations to the extent that we can look at adolescent family relations through new eyes.

Rosenbaum accomplishes this by showing us Floe's little sister, Sunny, now fully grown up, functioning as Floe's guardian. We see the slippage between the role of guardian/provider and parent in the constant struggle between the two characters once Floe has awakened. For instance;

"You can't go," Sunny says flatly while making shortbread cookies in the kitchen. (This is my sister now; meatloaf and shortbread cookies. Not an ounce of Venice Beach left in her.) "Jake's napping, I need you to babysit. Andrew's tennis partner just canceled, so we're going to play each other."

"Sunny, please, I've been sitting for Jake so much!" I've already done the five times I owed her for driving me to the Havajava Café that time, and more.

"Floe, that's what older siblings do," she says patiently.

"I'm not his *sibling*!" I explode. I close my eyes, "Look, Sunny, I love Jake, I really do, he's adorable, but I'm his aunt, not his sister."

"While I'm your guardian, you're his *de facto* sister," she says. (95)

Here, not only do we see the slippage of sibling relations, we can also see the issue of work within the family defamiliarized in order to view it anew. Like so many adolescents, it is assumed that Floe will simply do unpaid caretaking work so that her "parents" may go off and do something else. It is important to note that Sunny's position here (and throughout most of the book it remains so) is that Floe must take on the role of her child rather than her sibling in the familial order. Moreover, Sunny's desire is to have time away from the child in order to play tennis—she wants recreation time. She doesn't see, or at least doesn't admit to seeing, the contradiction inherent in curtailing Floe's recreation time for her own. Sadly, this is also a situation experienced by many adolescents.

After many fights on this subject, though, Sunny comes to a sense of understanding for Floe. This is shown when Sunny brings in someone else, Marissa (a girl from down the street), to watch the child, allowing Floe to have her own life away from the family.

"I can feed him before I go," I offer.
"No need," Marissa says, "I'll do it."
"Thanks, Mar," Sunny says. "There's a bottle in the fridge."

> "Thanks for coming, Marissa," I say awkwardly. "Usually I babysit but—"
>
> "You have a life," Sunny finishes.
>
> I look at her, but she's busy playing with Jake and Beau.
>
> "Right. But next time—"
>
> "We'll work it out, Floe."
>
> "Um, okay," I say, at a loss for words. (178)

In this way, Sunny and her husband get to have time away for recreation, and Floe gets to have her own life, as well. We can imagine that Marissa is being compensated in some way for her work caring for the child, or at very least seems happy to do so, something that was not even offered to Floe.

The ideological payoff for the reader is, of course, Sunny and Floe having a conversation while waiting for their parents to be unfrozen (once a cure for the disease is found). After a few moments of awkward conversation on the subject of their lives together since Floe's return, Sunny says of the foster parents who took her in when Floe and her own parents were frozen, "Losing you guys *was* really hard," she admits. "But the Tabers were great. They tried their best. They didn't deserve to be treated the way I treated them. And I told them that at your party" (240). The point of the estrangement emerges: the adolescent reader is meant to see the familial relationship between the adolescent and the family structure in new ways via Floe's journey, and in the end, to have more sympathy for the parents' point of view.

We can also see family as the point of estrangement in Mildred Ames's 1981 novel, *Anna to the Infinite Power*. In the novel, Anna Hart discovers that she is in fact a clone of a famous scientist. Her mother is the only other person in the family who knows. When the experiment comes to fruition, Anna's identity as a clone is brought to the attention of her family and their reactions are then to both other and to deal with the othering of Anna. Here, we can see the other coding relationship as that between a family and a child who is different, special. During one conversation between Graham (Anna's father) and Rowan (Anna's brother), we see them both working through their othering of Anna:

> "We'll probably get used to the idea in time," Rowan said.
> "If I had no part in it, I shouldn't feel guilty, now should I?"
> "Of course not."
> "Well, I try not to." Graham Hart gave a resigned sigh. "Your mother's right. The important thing now is Anna herself. Whatever she is, she's a human being, a person. Knowing how *I* feel, I can imagine how *she* feels, learning about her origin at this late date. We'll have to help her all we can, Rowan."
> "Sure, Dad," Rowan said, but his heart wasn't in the words. (64)

Would Graham have even had to make the statement that he could imagine how Anna felt if he didn't think of her as somehow nothuman? Her clone nature makes him doubt that she is a human to the point that he has to make a pronouncement that she is one to combat his doubts. Rowan, however, does not immediately fall in line with the attitude his father espouses. He wants to be away from her before even learning that she is in no way actually related to him by blood.

An interesting thing that happens in the defamiliarization depicted in this novel is that we also get to see Anna's own reactions. She grapples with ontological uncertainty. Anna's uncertainty as to her identity mirrors adolescence. Upon learning that she is, in fact, a clone, she asks, "They might as well tell me that I'm not me . . . that there isn't any me. And if there isn't any me, then who am I, this body I can see in the mirror? Am I the dead Anna Zimmerman living a second life? Are my thoughts only her thoughts? Who am I? What am I?" (41). Here, we can see Anna's concern over her identity mirroring that of many adolescents. "Which is the true me?" she wonders: them existing here, or the person she is supposedly patterned after? She is attempting to find the space that is uniquely her. The drive to other is so powerfully engrained in her that she is tempted to other herself—her clone nature creates a powerful break in her own narrative of self, and here we see her struggling with the dividing line between conception of self and othered self.

The defamiliarization of the family, though, is not the only thing that is examined via science fiction processes.

Taking Some Readings

One of the first things that any landing party does in a science fiction story is to take some readings. This means that the characters get out their sensing instruments and examine the area around their landing point, gathering more information and exploring their new environment. Here, I wish to do something very similar. I want to take a reading of a few YA science fiction texts to show in a more detailed way what I mean.

Robin Wasserman's 2008 novel, *Skinned*, is an example of the intersection of YA and feminist science fiction. In the novel, Lia Kahn wakes up in an artificial body after a terrible car accident. She is informed that she would have died, otherwise. Over the course of the narrative, she finds herself confronting many othered subjectivities and the disidentification of those around her. For a time, she tries to live the same life she did as a flesh-and-blood adolescent, but finds that almost no one will accept her that way. Members of the religious movement within the narrative even openly attack her in public, claiming that since she has been dead, being alive in the mechanical body is an abomination. She eventually meets a group of other adolescents who live in these mechanical bodies and she must make a choice—does she continue to attempt to pass in the life she had before the accident, or does she reject the organic bodied "orgs" and exist outside of the binary of mech versus org?

Here we have what Ostry and others might refer to as the problem of the posthuman body. She says, "The posthuman body is a metaphor for how foreign one's body feels during adolescence, as adolescents must discover themselves and reintegrate into their society" (238). Lia now has to define herself in much the same way Anna did in Ames's novel. She is on the border between the two ontologies of machine and human. Through the course of the novel and its 2009 sequel, *Crashed*, this is the primary point of contention: what is the difference between machines and humans? Lia's journey is not just one of self-discovery, but self-definition in a very literal sense.

Lia meets with this group, walking directly toward those whose othered status she shares. When she gets frustrated at their rejection of her orientation toward the organic, she says to Auden, the only organic her own age still talking to her, "This is why I didn't want to come" (237). We can see her attempting to other the mechs and ally herself with the organic. Immediately, though, Jude, the leader of the mechs says to her,

> Jude leaned forward. "Then why did you?"
> "None of your business."
> "Maybe you got bored pretending you still fit in to your tiny, claustrophobic org life," he suggested. "You're looking for a better way."
> "Better?" I sneered. "If this is so much better, if you're all so superior, then why doesn't *everyone* want to be a skinner?"[21] (237)

Here, she is directly addressing their ideological stance—what we might call the reversal of the other. Jude and his group have adopted a scapegoating rhetorical stance to gain power over those that devalue their subjectivity. Immediately, Jude responds,

> "We don't use that word here," Jude said quietly. "We're *mechs*. And proud of it."
> There was a long pause.
> "Sorry," I said, only because I felt like I had to. (237)

Lia apologizes for her former stance. It is here that we can see her begin to undo the rhetorical stance that she has been programmed with—the doubled consciousness of othering the mechs while being one herself because she still thinks of herself as an organic-bodied human. In many ways, this conversation codes the doubled consciousness that any young homosexual feels when confronted with the daunting possibility of coming out. It may also resonate in terms of race for some readers. Notice how, as with those situations, Lia's fallback ideological position is to identify with the dominant hegemony; alignment with the organic-bodied humans codes for alignment with white, heterosexual culture in many ways. Notice, too, the rhetorical identification moves that Jude and the other mechs have made to reclaim their power in that marginalized status. In encountering it, Lia has confronted the other and finds that it is her.

In the end, Lia accepts her status as the other—this is her move to power in Trites's sense of the term. At the end of the novel, Lia says,

> I was tired of pretending that nothing had changed. That even with an artificial body and a computer for a brain, I was still the same person I'd been before. Denial was exhausting. As was anger. Bargaining was useless. Depression was bottomless. I was tired of it all. Which meant I was ready to accept it. The new reality of nonlife after nondeath. *My* new reality. Lia Kahn is dead. I am Lia Kahn. Except, I finally realized, here's the thing. Maybe I'm not. (361)

As we can see, Lia has continued her dialogue with the other, even when she finds it to be herself. She notes that she has tried everything she can think of to defend that border between self and other that Hatty describes. In the end, she finds that she and the other are one, and that all her efforts to "vigilantly police" that border, as Hatty says, have been wasted time.

The social critical work of science fiction is to bring the reader to the encounter with the other. Much like Lia Kahn, we expect that there will be struggle, but we also recognize that this struggle is fruitful because readers thereby gain some insight into the mechanism of othering and how they have been constructed by it. We can see othering tackled in a similar way in Sylvia Engdahl's 1970 novel, *Enchantress from the Stars*. In this novel, we meet Elana, a teenager who is along with her father during his leave time from the Anthropological Service when an emergency call comes in. Along with Evrek, a somewhat older boy who is intended to be Elana's husband at some point in the future, Elana's father is sent to deal with a situation where a technologically advanced (though, we are shown, not as advanced as Elana's own culture) society, who refer to themselves as the Empire, has decided to colonize a planet with a population that is far less advanced than they are, called the Andrecians. Elana sneaks down with Evrek and her father and thus becomes entangled in the operation to thwart the Empire's efforts to take the planet from the native population. We meet Georyn, an Andrecian, and the youngest of four sons of a woodcutter, and Jarel, a medic assigned to the expeditionary force of the Empire sent to Andrecia to prepare it for colonization. Each of the characters gets whole sections as focalizer, and through this, the reader sees the situation from many different perspectives. It is primarily through Jarel, though, that othering is explored.

Early on, Jarel says of the people of Andrecia,

> It wasn't as if the original inhabitants of this world had any rights under the Charter. If they were anywhere near that level, the planet wouldn't have been chosen, but they were not. They were merely humanoid animals. It being Empire policy to avoid wiping out native species where possible, they would be granted tracts of land. Some of them might even prove trainable; there was always a labor shortage in a new colony. (20)

Of course, this kind of callous view of others is precisely Engdahl's point. She fully intends for us to be shocked by this way of thinking (and to draw immediate comparison to the rhetorics that circulated around America's removal of native nations from their lands in the mid- to late eighteen hundreds). Jarel's othering of the Andrecians is strongly tied to his subjectivity as a member of the Empire.

Engdahl also intends for us to watch Jarel's ideological stances change over the course of the novel. He goes from thoroughly othering the Andrecians to the complete opposite—understanding that they are no different from his own culture. Eventually Jarel gets the confirmation he desires about the Andrecians when Elana outs herself as being from a more technologically advanced civilization. "Then they *were* people, Jarel thought triumphantly. To a race that was far, far ahead of the Empire, even, the natives were people" (225). Of course, Jarel needed to see someone from another, more advanced culture as an example. In some ways, Elana's father is incorrect in thinking that the way to save the Andrecians from the Empire is to stay invisible from the people of the Empire. In the end, it is contact with Jarel just as much as contact with Georyn that saves Andrecia. Jarel's move of identification runs counter to the ideology of his culture (identifying more with Elana's long view of history than his own culture's shorter view, which tells people of the Empire that they are the pinnacle of evolution). He says of his own revelation, "There's nothing wrong with us as a people. . . . We are not decadent, not wicked, not on the wrong road! We are going somewhere after all. We are as far below *her* people as the natives are below us . . . but someday!" (262). Of course, his thinking is still in terms of "below" and "above," an orientation toward supremacy of one culture over another. The reader is left with the hope that someday, though, even that will fall away.

This is not to say that Elana, even coming from the civilization that we are told is more advanced than the Andrecians or the people of the Empire, has her own (though milder) othering to deal with. Her father tells her,

> "[O]ne of the first things you'll learn when you start working with these people is that they are fundamentally no different from other people you know. The fact that they are Younglings in terms of their culture does not mean that they are in any way childish as individuals." (73)

Having been trained by the Service, and having the status of senior agent, her father is much more experienced with encounters with "younger" civilizations (which those who exist in the community that supports the Service call "Younglings"). While the idea of using an age-metaphor to denote a hierarchy of knowledge seems somewhat counter to Engdahl's message, she explains that this is cultural ideology. She explains this particular ideological understanding of other peoples early on via a text that Elana is reading,

> It is by now a well known fact that the human peoples of the universes have similar histories—not that the specific details are similar, but the same patterns emerge on every home world. Each must pass through three stages: first, childhood, when all is full of wonder, when man admits that much is unknown to him, calling it "supernatural," yet believing. Then adolescence, when man discards superstition and reveres science, feeling that he has charted its realms and has only to conquer them— never dreaming that certain "supernatural" wonders should not be set aside, but understood. And at last, maturity, when the discovery is made that what was termed "supernatural" has been perfectly natural all along, and is in reality a part of the very science that sought to reject it . . . [ellipses in the original] (16)

We are meant in some ways to think of Evrek, Elana, and her father as superior because of their inclusive stance. They have this ideological concept of a hierarchy of cultures, a sort of conceptual ladder of achievement, and readily apply the term Youngling to those who have not reached the level that they have on this ladder. Here is a Burkean identification move writ large: an entire culture sees itself as more advanced than whole other cultures simply by the yardstick which they have determined. In some ways, this is Žižek's warning: that to theorize an awareness of ideology as freedom from ideological construction creates a problem for the one doing the theorizing. Those in the Anthropological Service are still constructed, and still on the ladder, but have conceived of themselves as being high enough on that ladder to judge other civilizations. One can theorize that an extension of Engdahl's concept would have Elana's family eventually coming into contact with another civilization that considers itself to be beyond her own. I believe that this is Engdahl's most social-critical tool of the narrative more so than any particular character's journey: a criticism of the concept of a ladder of civilization-achievement. In some ways, here is her critique of the concept of "first world" versus "third world" nations, cognitively estranged enough to make it easier for the reader to theorize.

Similar moves of othering and identification occur in Louise Lawrence's 1996 novel, *Dream-weaver*. In the novel we meet Troy Morrison, the teenaged son of one of the mission commanders aboard the colonization ship the *Exodus 27*. This is his first space mission, and so in his journey we see much of the othering that the adolescent experiences in terms of experience. In the novel, we also encounter Eth, a prepubescent female dream-weaver-in-training of the planet Arbroth (which is the very planet that *Exodus 27* is bound for). The mission of *Exodus 27* is to deliver the colonists, all kept on board in a state of suspended animation for the long journey, to Arbroth. Because of contact with Eth and other Arbrothans via their dream-weaving techniques, that mission is thwarted, and the colonists are convinced/threatened into finding another planet to inhabit.

The novum in this novel, the Dream-weavers, we discover, is a society who polices the feelings and relations of their people, shaping the dreams of those who reside within. We are tempted in some ways to judge the Arbrothans as a "lesser" civilization, if we were to borrow the concept of a cultural ladder from Engdahl's novel. They seem to be a preindustrial revolution agricultural-based society. It is not until we discover that there is a great deal of technological sophistication kept under disguise as a reaction against a past catastrophe that we are forced to reconsider this stance. Dream-weaving is their answer to that catastrophe: weapons are no longer required if the society can be soothed via their subconscious before any conflicts even break out. One of the characters, Cable, puts it this way while teaching Eth about her ability:

> "Who controls the dream controls the man," said Cable. "And that's what your work consists of. A dream-weaver unravels people's problems, roots out resentment or aggression or whatever other negative drive is operating in a particular man or woman, and restores the sense of their interrelationships. You dream-weave for the peace of this planet." (56)

The dream-weaver functions as preemptive psychologist, going into the person's subconscious and manipulating their thoughts and feelings. If the subconscious is a language, the dream-weaver functions as editor. The othering works both ways. We see reactions to the differences in both cultures. Troy is quite unhappy with the colonists' mission. The idea of arriving on some new planet and taking it from the native population infuriates him, "Troy's fists clenched. This should not be allowed to happen, he thought. That world belonged to its native population, not to Mr. Guttenham or anyone else on board this ship. They had no right to take it for themselves" (26). He has a very developed sense that, no matter how terrible things are for people on Earth (the green message of the novel in terms of the future it posits for Earth is unmistakable), taking a planet from its native population is wrong. Here, Troy begins his journey in the place Jarel arrives at by the end of Engdahl's novel.

We can see something of the ideological underpinning of the colonists' belief that they have the right to take Arbroth from its native population in an exchange Troy has with his parents while the ship is still en route:

> "Why bother?" asked Verity. "There are rules regarding alien life forms encountered in deep space. We avoid them! So I want her off this ship at the first opportunity!"
>
> "You can hardly evict someone made of thin air!" said Troy. "And Eth's as human as we are, Mom. Put her back on Arbroth in her physical

body, and you wouldn't think twice about hiring her as a domestic servant when we actually land!"

"She'd be lovely to look at, too," murmured his father. (113)

To her credit, Verity, Troy's mother, immediately turns on her husband for his sexist remark. However, she does not deny her son's accusation. Verity's conception of anything other than humans is that they are something to be feared. Eth represents danger to her; contact is a thing to be avoided at all costs. Notice for Troy's father, Eth represents the exotic body to seduce; the other as sexual alternative (his attention in this passage made all the more horrible when one remembers that Eth has not yet reached puberty).

The othering that results from this encounter, though, is not one sided. Eth's dream encounters with the crew of the *Exodus 27*, and Troy in specific, leave her having to describe those who are aboard to people of her culture.

> "He wasn't like us at all," said Eth. "His skin was pale as the underbelly of a slime crawler, and his hair was the color of ripe grain. He wore a silver suit, and his eyes were blue."
>
> "Blue eyes?" said Arlynn. "How can anyone have blue eyes, Eth?
>
> "I told you he was odd," said Eth. (11)

Eth is reduced to having to find metaphors to describe Troy. Notice, though, that to her credit, while she does find Troy odd, her othering is not power based. Troy is not a threat to be stamped out in her mind. Even when others of her culture who are somewhat warlike take up the description, it is not the same as when Troy's family does. A character named Vashilan says of Eth's dream, "If these dreams of hers be real, and if they are linked to those former events, then think what they may portend. She has seen an army frozen in transit, pale skinned warriors from the stars!" (31). This is something of an odd moment of othering; Vashilan assumes that the colonists and crew of *Exodus 27* are warriors, that their intent is not peaceful. We know him to be correct. However, he is assuming, here, with very little proof. This is othering the same way that the humans' assumption that Eth is a threat is. In this case, though, he is correct in his assumption.

That is not to say that her culture does not develop an attack response to the colonists—they do. However, we might even think of their defense as somewhat more enlightened than the colonists would have mounted in that the Arbrothans defend themselves using psychic ability instead of conventional weaponry. The goal is to scare the colonists away from the planet in order to avoid war and possible enslavement, not to destroy them.

In the end, Troy recognizes that "it was what they would all have to do, Troy supposed—change their thinking, change their ways, and learn to work together" (228). The colonists have made the right decision to not invade Eth's home world and now must face the consequences of that decision. The end result is a society faced with hard choices in their future, but choices that do not radically other an entire people by disempowering them (or even killing them). The colonists arrive at a space where othering is still possible, and likely, but no longer includes the possibility of invasion and/or genocide.

A Critical Vantage Point

Science fiction for young adults is particularly useful for examining the processes of othering, as well as conceiving of the encounter with the other. Freedman maintains that science fiction is inherently dialogic in its nature, due to the tension between cognition (our sense of the "real world" that takes place around us being at least somewhat similar to the "real world" of the text) and estrangement (the radical alterity suggested by the novum or multiple linked novae) (16). This tension creates in science fiction texts an inherent tendency to be *critical* texts, as well. It is the dialogue that is important, I believe, not necessarily whatever the proposed answer might be in each individual text. I note again Jean Baudrillard's assertion that "from one order of simulacra to another, the tendency is certainly toward the reabsorption of the distance, of this gap that leaves room for an ideal or critical projection" (121–22). Science fiction, he says, can no longer be thought of as "unreal." In a postmodern world, where the map of the world is the same size and shape as the world, covering it, then science fiction is not merely critical of the "real world." It also maps and is mapped. As Adam Roberts reminds us, the narratives of spaceships are often far more fascinating to us than space missions carried out by flesh-and-blood astronauts (154). He suggests, in other words, that science fiction may not be as useful a vehicle to gain distance on reality for critical endeavors as many other theorists believe it to be. Still, as Žižek points out, though, understanding that a space seemingly outside of ideology is already mapped should not stop us from stepping in to such a space and carrying out examinations of ideology, anyway. We must not simply throw our hands up and reject the critical endeavor altogether. We can find a place from which to examine ideology so long as we recognize that space is already "mapped"—is already ideological, itself. Science fiction can help us to problematize the process of othering as it occurs in the ontological interplay between discourses of "being-ness" and subjectivity. Instead of thinking of science fiction as an escape hatch, to borrow some of its terminology, from ideological constructions, we can conceive of the work of science fiction instead as a critical vantage point, as higher ground that is still on the map, but from which a clearer view of the land is gained, in a metaphoric sense. As I have said, I think this is an absolutely essential topic of discussion for adolescents as they develop their critical awareness of the discourses that surround them.

"The Treatment for Stirrings": Dystopian Literature for Adolescents

The word "utopia" comes from the 1516 text of the same name by Thomas More. While it immediately suggests its opposite, it wasn't until 1868 that John Stuart Mill first officially used the term "dystopia." As Wang Xiaolan points out, from the beginning both terms have a history as an adjective and as a name for a literary genre. This dual sense of each word has, over time, created a certain amount of slippage between them. In this chapter we will discuss the specific history of the genre of literature that is called "dystopia" with an eye toward how that genre has evolved into the current form it takes in young adult literature, and also with the goal of helping to shore up some of the aforementioned definitional slippage.

Unlike the science fiction text, which is inherently critical toward the dominant culture's conceptions of othering, the utopian text is bound up in further entrenching the power relationships that already exist, according to Keith Booker, a major theorist of dystopian literature. One must always ask "whose idea of the perfect world are we looking at?" when dealing with a utopian text. Dystopian literature, though, "is specifically that literature which situates itself in direct opposition to utopian thought, warning against the potential negative consequences of arrant utopianism" (Booker, *Dystopian Literature* 3). Dystopian literature is in direct dialogue with utopian thinking. Booker goes on to say:

> It also indicates why so many modern thinkers have become suspicious of utopian thought, fearing that such visions can ultimately work only to the advantage of the status quo. Still, utopian visions of ideal alternatives have long formed an important part of criticisms of contemporary society. (*Dystopian Literature* 3)

In this chapter, I wish to demonstrate the ways that dystopian texts for young adults explore subjectivity. Like Carrie Hintz and Elaine Ostry, I believe that

> Children's and young adult utopias are in particular need of sustained study for two reasons. First of all, there is a long tradition of thinking of childhood itself as utopian, a space and time apart from the corruption of everyday adult life. The second reason is the unique function that utopianism and utopian writing plays in children's socialization and education. (5)

I would extend this to include dystopian texts, as well. In this chapter, I will show how many scholars have attempted to critique dystopian texts for young adults and/or children via an orientation toward hope. I want to explore the ways that we might form a somewhat more sophisticated way of looking at these texts than the presence or rejection of hope. After initially establishing a definition based on various theoretical explorations, I will provide a brief overview of the literary history of the dystopia before moving into my analysis of those texts that best help me illustrate the underlying structure that creates a critical trajectory for the dystopian text for young adults.

Jack Zipes believes that "it would be misleading to argue that every story written for children is utopian, or to assert that there is an 'essential' utopian nature to writing for young people" (ix). Hintz and Ostry make a similar argument, saying, "It is impossible to rely on genre, for example, to establish a text's utopian nature, since the form of utopian works varies" (3). I disagree; I believe we not only can rely on genre, we must. We must begin to parse through these texts and determine some generic tendency if we are to effectively categorize these texts for use in classrooms (or for recommendation to patrons of libraries) with use-to-the-reader in mind. Again, though, I wish to make clear that I do not intend such categorization for purposes of establishing some hierarchy of artistic value. Instead, I intend this to be a sorting of tools into order so that they may be used efficiently. Beebee's concept of use value of genres helps in discussing this genre, especially when we examine how use value intersects with explorations of subjectivity.

As I will investigate later in this chapter, though, there have been many theorists who wish to explore the genre in terms of its orientation toward hope. Fredric Jameson believes that we must get beyond looking for a sense of hope versus a lack of hope for the future as the primary goal of the text. Instead, he wants critics to consider an exploration of subjectivity as the primary theme of dystopia. He says,

> I believe, however, that it is best to consider this particular dilemma a part of the Utopian debate in a new sector of thematics which we have not yet touched on, namely that of subjectivity . . . in other words, the question of the formation of subjectivities, and that of the problems posed by their death and succession, by the generations and the relationship of the later classes of subjects to the institutions of Utopia laid in place by their predecessors . . . This is probably the area in which the modern concern with freedom, which replaces the older Utopian preoccupation with happiness, can most adequately be grasped. (166–67)

Freedom to or freedom from, as Margaret Atwood's character puts it in her novel, *The Handmaid's Tale*, thus becomes the central focus of inquiry rather than hope. When freedom becomes the primary critical point, then the formation of subjectivity at the hands of societal pressure, the ISA/RSA cycle explored in chapter 1, is the direction we should be looking.

This chapter, then, has a narrower scope than the previous chapter. I intend to examine only novels published in the twentieth and twenty-first centuries that I identify as young adult dystopian texts. While I mention some dystopian film in the brief history section below, I have chosen not to include them in the analysis portions of the chapter that come after.[1] I also do not intend to examine attempts to create utopian communities in the empirical world in this chapter. I mention this because, as Zipes points out in his foreword, there have been many other real-world attempts at utopian communities. Some of these end in a dystopian community being born. The scope of this book, though, is specifically in YA dystopian literature. I am not interested so much in the ways that these real-world communities came into being or eventually fell into difficulty. I leave that project to the many other scholars working in that field within utopian studies. I want to begin this chapter by looking at those critiques that say utopian/dystopian texts are delineated by their orientation toward hope.

"A Negative Cousin"

Lymon Tower Sargent argues that "young adult dystopias are remarkably similar to those written for adults" (230). This is to say that there is far less difference between dystopian works intended for adults and those intended for a young audience than one might find between other genres and their young adult counterparts. However, when examining the constituent parts of a dystopian narrative written for any audience, it is important to have a base definition to work from. Unfortunately, this proves somewhat difficult. As Thomas Moylan suggests in his book, *Scraps of the Untainted Sky*, there has been a great deal of gradation in the writing of the genre, as well as much nuanced criticism over the years. This leaves anyone examining the genre with many varying terms to parse, such as "anti-utopia" and "critical dystopia," to name a few. Here, I wish to confine the examination to one category of works.[2] In order to simplify for purposes of keeping in mind this book's goal, which is to help the reader understand the differences between science fiction for young people and dystopian literature intended for a young adult audience, I offer a stripped-down definition from which to proceed. Bradford and colleagues suggest of dystopias that

> such literary works dispense with the state as the centre of social control and replace it with the totalizing political-economic machinery of the hegemonic system (and not simply the state, party, corporation, religion or other undemocratic power) that brings exploitation, terror and misery to society. (144)

Notice that Bradford and his colleagues do not say that dystopia requires a futuristic setting. Instead, the dystopian text focuses on totalitarianism within a given community and the responses from the people within that community, a point I will return to later in this chapter. Fredric Jameson suggests that

> The critical dystopia is a negative cousin of the Utopia proper, for it is in the light of some positive conception of human social possibilities that its effects are generated and from Utopian ideals its politically enabling stance derives. Yet if one reserves the term dystopia for works of this kind, then Orwell's works must be characterized in a markedly different way and by a distinctive generic terminology: I propose to characterize them as anti-Utopian given the way in which they are informed by a central passion to denounce and to warn against Utopian programs in the political realm. (198–99)

Jameson is agreeing with Booker in a sense about the dialogue between the utopian concept and the dystopian concept, but I think he is employing the terminology somewhat strangely. I agree that some care must be taken: if hope is our only criterion for utopian writing, and these texts do not provide hope, then it is true that we must define Orwellian works as anti-utopian. However, I disagree that hope is the primary characteristic on which to base the definition of the genre. I prefer to avoid the situation in which we are forced to say, "because text A lacks hope, it is therefore dystopian." Such thinking leads to a false understanding of the genre and the work it performs.

Instead, I prefer to look at what dystopian texts are *doing*. The use value cannot be defined merely in terms of the fact that they provide a lack of hope—that seems nonsensical. Instead, dystopian texts perform social critical work—a use value—that allows the reader to question the polyvalent relationships between subjectivity and power. Dystopian authors create texts that show us a worst-case scenario. I maintain that in dystopian works, especially those for young adults, we see the author functioning as a cultural theorist in the subjunctive mode I mentioned in chapter 1. The effect is often a chilling warning-by-hyperbole of what might come if we are not careful. These are works in which society is shown in totalitarian extremes. If the author's intention is to warn us of what might come, then the most logical way to examine that is in this subjunctive mode or theory—or, more specifically, theoretically informed fiction writing. This is all true; however, I do not believe that the *primary* work of the text is found only in this sense of warning (i.e., an orientation toward a lack of hope).

As I explored in chapter 1, Karen Sands and Marietta Frank remind us,

> Although utopias present a "perfect" world, at least in the viewpoint of the authors who created them, the premise behind both utopias and dystopias is essentially pessimistic. In the case of utopias, their very creation assumes a presently imperfect world with the goal of allowing some escape from it; dystopias generally posit that our current world

is doomed to metamorphosize [*sic*] into the very opposite of utopia. In either instance, the likelihood of never reaching a utopic situation is very high. (78)

The presence or lack of hope, however, is a primary component of such a definition. Sands and Frank rightly point out that often readers are left with a sense of unease about the future. This is what is intended. However, with a particular set of theoretical tools that I will posit here, I think we can see much deeper into the structures of these texts. While Hintz and Ostry, as well as Bradford and colleagues, point toward hope as the primary foundation of utopian conceptions, I believe we have to make our examination criteria more sophisticated. This is especially the case with dystopian writing for young adults.

Peter Hollindale says that any children's author "must construct childhood from an amalgam of personal retrospect, acquaintance with contemporary children, and an acquired set of beliefs as to what children are, and should be, like" (12). Childhood is a conceptual map laid over biological facts. It is, in that sense, ideologically constructed, as is any concept of a utopia. Childhood itself is often theorized as a utopia that exists until adults intervene (Sands and Frank 78). This conservative, pastoral-driven impulse is present in the dystopian narrative. Patricia Warrick agrees, believing that dystopian fiction "generally demonstrates more of a conservative than futuristic orientation; it longs for a return to the simple, natural world of the past" (219). Through the power of repressive strategies, the regime within the narrative tries to recreate the citizen subject of their society as childlike. As Hintz and Ostry explain,

> [W]e discovered that utopias predominate in children's literature, whereas dystopias are far more common in young adult literature. This is hardly surprising. It reflects the way in which young children are rarely depicted to themselves as suffering, especially collectively. Furthermore, adolescence frequently entails traumatic social and personal awakening.

> The adolescent comes to recognize the faults and weaknesses of his or her society, and rebels against it. (9)

In essence, utopian writing is the predominant mode of texts intended for children because of our societal impulse to put them into a safe space, to arrest their growth. The dystopian work pervades adolescent literature because of our equally strong societal need to push the adolescent from their state of in-between-ness to a state of adulthood. Hintz and Ostry go on to assert:

> [D]ystopia can act as a powerful metaphor for adolescence. In adolescence, authority appears oppressive, and perhaps no one feels more under surveillance than the average teenager. The teenager is on the brink of adulthood: close enough to see its privileges but unable to enjoy them. The comforts of childhood fail to satisfy. The adolescent craves more power and control and feels the limits on his or her freedom intensely. (9–10)

I will explore this surveillance more closely later in this chapter. Indeed, it forms a primary point of what we might call a grammar of dystopian writing. "These [dystopian] worlds spell the death of childhood as a secure, cherished state, deliberately calling constructions of 'childness' and 'adultness' into serious question" (Sambell, "Carnivalizing" 250).

Again, as Ostry and Hintz point out, the comforts of childhood are the very things that are removed for the work to be dystopian. In utopian writing, the state is often engaged in infantilizing its entire population, but without the sense of benevolent power often associated with the parental figure in the utopia-as-childhood construction. Consider for a moment the case in Lowry's *The Giver*. It bears repeating that the infantilized state of the populace is produced by the strict codes and mores, and this uncomplicated state is often seen as utopia by readers. Sands and Frank remind us, though, that there is little hope for the subject to change or gain agency within that system. There is no hope in such a situation. Bradford and colleagues say that a critical dystopia, as they deploy the term, does not give up on "hope despite the dystopian worlds they depict" (139).[3] The "lack of hope" they describe in the text actually stands in to give the reader hope. The reader sees the difference between the text world and his/her own empirical world, which can call the reader to action: perhaps, the reader thinks, there is a chance to avert a world such as the text presents. As Bullen and Parsons say of such narratives, "In this way, the act of reading becomes the impetus to action" (38). The point of such a narrative is to inspire the (implied) child reader to action. This is accomplished through the urge to disidentify, in a Burkean sense, with the type of regime depicted in the text. "We need to pass through the critical dystopias of today to move toward a horizon of hope" (Baccolini 521). In reaching for that horizon, the focalizer, so long infantilized by the repressive regime, moves into adolescence—a breaking away from childhood into self-reliance and responsibility. Rather than believing that hope versus lack of hope is the primary criteria for determining if a text is utopian or dystopian, though, I instead want to point out that "the assumption that in a dystopian world human beings must strive for a form of subjective agency pervades children's literature" (Bradford 29). There is a reason this is the case: the primary focus of the dystopian work is such an exploration of subjectivity. The intent is not only to explore the construction of subjectivity in the face of naked abuses of power at the hands of the ruling regime, but also to provide examples of agency in such situations.

Sambell says that,

> Above all, children's dystopias seek to violently explode blind confidence in the myth that science and technology will bring about human "progress." They achieve this by working through the application of science in worst-case scenarios, demonstrating that it can be used to bring about oppressive, inhuman and intolerable regimes, rather than "civilized" ones. ("Carnivalizing" 247–48)

Utopias always fail, falling into dystopias. This is because one person's concept of perfection and peace may not be another's. Because of this, in dystopian literature for young adults, hope versus lack of hope is not the defining characteristic. Instead, these texts have at their core explorations of subjectivity relating to the power of the child. As Sambell asserts, we must examine the way that "the dystopian form for children is used to make serious and daunting comment on where we are really going as a society and, worse, what we will be like when we get there" ("Carnivalizing" 247).[4] Dystopian texts fill a gap between what we see as our current situation and the future (Zipes ix). Again, these texts are not only critical statements, but a call to action on the part of the reader, even if that action is only to begin to think more critically about the relationships between power and subjectivity that circulate within his or her current society. We can say that:

> On the most obvious level, then, the dystopia didactically foregrounds social and political questions by depicting societies whose structures are horrifyingly plausible exaggerations of our own. Dystopian authors predominantly teach by negative example, "making the familiar strange" in order to shock and frighten readers into recognition of the dire need to question official culture and to expose the corruption of the present adult world that could plausibly lead to such bleak and intolerable futures. (Sambell, "Carnivalizing" 248)

Because the dystopian text is a highly critical one, any dystopian text for young adults will come into direct conflict with the didactic impulse of society. When there is this overlap between the truly dystopian and genre for young people, we can see that at some point (as with science fiction) there will be an impulse to reabsorb the critical subject. "Whereas the 'adult' dystopia's didactic impact relies on the absolute, unswerving nature of its dire warning, the expression of moral meaning in the children's dystopia is often characterized by degrees of hesitation, oscillation and ambiguity" (Sambell, "Presenting" 164).

Reviewing Subjectivity

In chapter 1, I explored a model for social formation of subjectivity based on the intersection of theories by Althusser, Foucault, and Burke. While Burkean theory forms the core of my examination of science fiction, it is Althusser and Foucault who provide the basis for my explanation of dystopian literature. I will refer here, as well, to Trites's concept of adolescent literature as a literature of social pressure, an ISA unto itself, in order to explain how dystopian literature for young people can be used to subvert the didactic drive normally associated with these types of texts.

As I suggested earlier, Burkean identification through the social lens of the work of Althusser and Foucault is the primary way in which the state monitors normative ideological formation of the subject in these fictions. Dystopian works attempt to make this system transparent. Authors of these types of texts are functioning as cultural theorists to show how the state first confines (Foucauldian surveillance) and then defines (Althusserian structures) the citizen. When we examine this genre we are left with a series of texts that not only show the various means any state might employ to force identification with officially sanctioned figures, but also how this same strategy is used to create figures that the subject is supposed to scapegoat.

Trites reminds us that "power is even more fundamental to adolescent literature than growth" (x). If the subject wanders too far from the ISA cycle, she/he falls into the jurisdiction of the RSAs—starting first with the policing entities, then the judicial system, and finally moving to whatever form of incarceration the culture practices. The adolescent, in negotiating the extremely complex process of subject formation at the hands of the ISAs, seemingly has the choice to conform or to dissent, thereby moving outside the ISAs and into the realm of the RSAs, where violence becomes socially viable for the state as a means to move the subject back toward the cycle of ISAs (Trites 3–7). The apparatuses in place to distribute the various polyvalent discourses of power that shape our society always have the adolescent under surveillance. These apparatuses are ready to apply corrective power in a continuum of force all the way from a casual verbal intervention to violence.

We see, then, in dystopian texts intended for young adults, a metaphorization of the movement from childhood to adolescence. More often than not, the YA novel seeks to reassert the state's dominance over the individual through both repression and formation via surveillance. As Trites argues, while some characters seem to gain power within the structure of the novel, in the end it is most often the state that gains control by normalizing the adolescent character via the narrative. These texts show the various power discourses at work on the adolescent as he or she moves from metaphoric childhood "utopia" to metaphoric adolescent "dystopia." The usefulness of this genre is that it shows more clearly the ways that society constructs the subject (in this case, the child or adolescent); it makes the often-invisible formative discourses visible by metaphor.

A History of Violence

While by no means exhaustive, here I would like to briefly trace the inception and development of dystopian writing for adults and for adolescents. No attempt to list every work has been made, but instead many of the most often cited texts are listed for each decade.

While there is a long and rich literary history of utopian texts, as well as a long history of attempts to create utopia in real-world settings, in this chapter, I wish to examine the dystopian as I have conceived of it. Going all the way back to Plato's *Republic*, we can see elements of what Karl Mannheim asserts in 1929's *Ideology and Utopia*: all conceptions of utopia are ideological in nature. Plato, like all writers who propose utopia in fiction (or in real-world settings) that come after him, is making decisions about who gets included in utopia and who does not. This means that both at the time of the utopia's inception as well as throughout its existence, certain subjectivities are selected for and others excluded. In Plato's case, it is the writer or "poet" who is excluded, but each iteration of utopia that comes after effectively polices its boundaries using ideology. In short, one person's utopia is another's hell. Each utopian concept always already contains within it a dystopian impulse. We must recognize that dystopian writing has always been contained in the utopian texts that come before Jack London's *The Iron Heel* (1908) or Yevgeny Zamyatin's novel *We* (1921).

We might pose these early dystopian works by London and Zamyatin as responses to the Russian Revolution of 1905. London's text follows hot on the heels of these events, and Zamyatin wrote his novel as a response to his experiences in both the Revolution of 1905 as well as the Revolution of 1917, which led to the institution of the Soviet state.[5] I am not intending to negate H. G. Wells's contribution to the dystopian genre by pointing to London and Zamyatin as the forerunners. In this case, I am, instead, saying that I believe there is a difference between a text in which the main character has lived within the dystopia all his life and is attempting to move outside of it (as is the case with London's Avis Everhard within the Oligarchy, and with Zamyatin's D-503 within the OneState) and a character who arrives there from outside (as is the case with H. G. Wells's Graham, who arrives in London 203 years after going into his "trance" in *When the Sleeper Wakes*). Although there are many works that precede these that are by turns dystop*ic*, being set after disasters or being explorations of future societies by those who travel there from some other space or time, we do not get what I call truly dystopian works until London and Zamyatin.[6]

From 1931 through 1962, many of the seminal works of this genre are published. Aldous Huxley's *Brave New World* is published in 1931 and George Orwell's *1984* in 1949, both of which serve to solidify the dystopian novel into the form I am describing here. Ray Bradbury publishes *Fahrenheit 451* in 1951. Ayn Rand publishes *Anthem* in 1961. Anthony Burgess publishes both *A Clockwork Orange* and *The*

Wanting Seed in 1962. It is within these novels that the idea of the state that controls its population with promises of taking care of them benevolently arises. These texts show how the state then inevitably fails to make good on its promise, opting for control instead of care.

After this there is an explosion of dystopian works for adults. In this period from the 1970s through the 1990s, the dystopian work is used to examine the patriarchy as the seemingly benevolent state repressing people in the name of "their own good." At least two of these works occur during the period of time when second-wave feminism was giving way to third wave. This period of time also marks the beginning of the backlash against feminism that Susan Faludi theorizes. In 1971, George Lucas adapts his student film, *THX 1138*, into a full-length motion picture of the same name. William F. Nolan's novel *Logan's Run* becomes the 1976 film of the same name. Terry Gilliam's film *Brazil* is released in 1985. Most notable among the dystopian works of the 1970s and 1980s are Monique Wittig's *Les Guérillères* in 1969 (with the English translation available in the United States in 1971), *The Handmaid's Tale* by Margaret Atwood in 1985, and *The Gate to Women's Country* by Sherri S. Tepper in 1988.

Since the 1990s, as the third wave of feminism expanded, and as Gay and Lesbian Studies were established as legitimate academic fields, the dystopian work has become even more likely to explore repressive regimes in the narrative in relation to those who live with repressed subjectivities in the empirical world outside the text. It is also the case that, in a post-9/11 world, the dystopian text has become a discourse for authors to highlight concerns over how technology and surveillance affect individual liberty. Matthew Stadler publishes his novel *The Sex Offender* in 1994. Kit Reed publishes *Thinner Than Thou* in 2004. Ninni Holmqvist publishes *The Unit* in 2006 (with the English translation available in the United States in 2008). Steven Spielberg loosely adapts Philip K. Dick's 1956 short story "The Minority Report" into a film of the same title in 2002. Alfonso Cuarón adapts P. D. James's 1992 novel, *The Children of Men*, into a film of the same title in 2006, and Trent

Reznor (Nine Inch Nails) releases a concept album set in a dystopian future entitled "Year Zero" in 2007.

In terms of dystopian works for children and young adults, there are many examples of postapocalyptic works, for those scholars that accept such works as dystopian, but fewer that fit into the definition of dystopian literature that I give here. Early on, the dystopian impulse tends to be merely one part of the text. For instance, in *Watership Down* (1972) the rabbits must travel through Efrafa and its dictator's brutal treatment before arriving at their promised utopia. William Golding's *Lord of the Flies* (1954) comes close to the definition of dystopian literature for young people I advance in this book, in that the boys must decide what type of society they wish to create; however, the period of time they spend under the control of the Hunters regime is fairly limited, and the boys clearly remember a time before their time on the island.

The dystopian impulse in works for children and young adults, though, truly begins with George Orwell who, in 1946, published *Animal Farm*. Here the anthropomorphized animal so familiar to children's literature becomes the citizen of a repressive regime. Although there might be some debate as to whether or not this novel is YA, I believe that it is. We can clearly see within it a problematization of the safe space of childhood—the benevolent dictatorship (read that "parents") is shown to be beneficial only for the dictator. While this is often categorized as a children's text, students frequently tend to encounter it in middle or high school, a move that would highlight the subject's moving out of the safe space of childhood.

For a short time, the areas of adult dystopian literature and those set aside for young adults overlapped. While Orwell, Bradbury, Huxley, and Burgess may have meant for their novels to be consumed by adults, they are often read by young adults because of their classification as science fiction, which, as I explored in chapter 2, was often defined as an adolescent genre. The various counterculture movements of the 1960s were especially receptive to the dystopian novels meant for adults published from the 1940s and 1950s. The 1960s, then, are the era when dystopian literature becomes the science fiction of the classroom, for both the high school and college level.

As I discuss below, *The Chocolate War* (1974) is a dystopian exploration of subject formation at the hands of a repressive regime (in this case, high school administration run amuck). The era also sees the publication of John Christopher's 1970 novel *The Guardians*, as well as Monica Hughes's *The Tomorrow City* in 1978. All of these novels involve some power (a computer, a priest, etc.) willing to engage in ruthless behavior toward the populations they control to maintain order.

While 1980s young adult literature is littered with postapocalyptic novels often confused with dystopian literature, the actual high points of YA dystopian lit are concerned with repressive regimes. Tom Brown publishes *Red Zone* in 1980. Todd Strasser's 1981 novel, *The Wave* (as I will explore later in this chapter), shows, like Cormier's earlier, how high school can be seen as a dystopian society. Robert Westall publishes *Futuretrack 5* in 1983, and John Tully publishes *Natfact 7* in 1984, both meditations on how utopian peace can seemingly only be maintained by brutal injustice.

Rigid social stratification is often at the center of the YA dystopian novels published in the 1990s. The 1990s also saw the publication of the novel that defines YA dystopian literature in many ways, Lois Lowry's 1993 novel, *The Giver*, which I will also discuss later in this chapter. Robert Swindel's *Daz 4 Zoe* comes out in 1990. Margaret Peterson Haddix's *Among the Hidden* is published in 1998, and in Sonia Levitin's *The Cure* from 1999, the main character's "cure" for having an emotional reaction is that there is danger in diversity. In each of these novels, the characters are kept from diversity by the rigid stratification of their society—the seeming perfection of their existence covers up gaps in power and privilege.

In the twenty-first century thus far, the YA dystopian novel seems to be about transgressing rigid social boundaries. While all of these protagonists, Daz, Luke, and Gemm 16884, are all in various ways prevented from overthrowing the social order, or content to wait until their chance to affect change, the adolescent protagonists of the twenty-first century more often resemble Jonas 1119 from Lowry's novel: they move right into their roles as revolutionaries. Jeanne DuPrau's *The City of Ember* was published in 2003, and Scott Westerfeld's *Uglies* in 2005.[7]

Depictions of State Apparatuses

In order to show these issues more clearly, I will examine them one by one, through example. First, I wish to show the ISA/RSA cycle as it appears in dystopian works for a young audience via examples from the novels *The Bar Code Tattoo*, *Among the Hidden*, and *City of Ember*. Next, I will demonstrate how surveillance functions in dystopian works for young adults with examples from the novels *The Maze Runner* and *Unwind*. Finally, I will examine *The Giver* in detail in order to show how these things work in concert with one another.

The way that the ISA cycle most often manifests itself in dystopian literature intended for young adults is when characters enforce social norms on other characters as though they were unquestionable, as if the given social norm is somehow a universalized truth, or an ethical absolute.

For example, this in an interaction in Suzanne Weyn's *The Bar Code Tattoo*. The novel follows Kayla Reed, who is about to turn seventeen, the age at which someone may get a bar code tattoo. These tattoos combine all the relevant identification methods and records that make up a person's life into one single UPC code tattooed onto the body. However, in the course of the narrative, the tattoo goes from being a helpful convenience that makes things like shopping easier to becoming a mandatory procedure. People who seem to have done nothing wrong are suddenly persecuted for information contained in their records that they are unaware of. Eventually, all those who don't have them are faced with only one choice: resist or comply. Kayla chooses to resist and goes on the run.

Early in the novel, there are warnings that things might go wrong with the coding process. Kayla's neighbor, Gene, who is a postal employee, says to her, "One French guy, though, told me his life had gone downhill fast once he got his. *Undesireable* was the word he used. He said, 'It's like I turned into an *undesireable* overnight.' Gene shrugged, as if the subject had begun to hurt his head and he wanted to get rid of it" (28). Despite all of his misgivings, Gene eventually shows Kayla that he has the tattoo, "I hope there's nothing too awful in there, because I got one. Had to or be fired" (29). Even though this is a technology designed for convenience, already there are consequences should someone wish to resist. Gene believes he will be fired from his job should he decide to not get the tattoo. Not long after this conversation, which proves to be his last with Kayla, Gene is dead. We are never quite sure, but there is a lingering feeling that perhaps he was killed for not hiding his resistance.

To establish the ISA's power, dystopian texts demonstrate some sort of internalization process; that is, some sort of pressure that is exerted on a main character on the part of someone else who is not a recognized authority of the state. In other words, a parent, priest, or friend must clearly show a desire to push the character in a certain direction that aligns with the desire of the state's ideology. In a very clear example of this, Amber, one of Kayla's friends, puts pressure on her to get the bar code tattoo: "'Not getting it?' Amber shouted incredulously. 'You can be as paranoid and suspicious as you like about it, but you have to realize that there's nothing you can do without a 'too! Nothing! For one thing, they don't give out any other kind of license anymore. No 'too, no license'" (32). Amber is horrified at the idea that Kayla may decide to not comply. The rhetorical choices Amber makes about citizenship itself are telling: she warns Kayla that there will be no way to gain legitimate identification without the tattoo. The literal writing of identity on the body and the visible sign of compliance with ideology are all combined into this sign of the bar code tattoo. Once more, readers are being made aware of the tattooing of numbers on the victims of the Holocaust and the cold efficiency of their identification and circumscription of rights.[8]

What is more interesting to me, though, is how Amber is attempting to push Kayla back into compliance. Amber lets Kayla know that she is aware of her suspicions. Amber also provides us with an interesting insight into why the ISA internalization of pressure/power works: she says to Kayla that whether these suspicions are right or wrong, she has succumbed to pressure because of her desire to remain active within society because her compliance is contingent on ability to still function. Amber doesn't say in this particular passage if she agrees with the ideology or not; she merely states why she complied. The strength of her reaction leads us to see what so often pervades discussions between people, as well: Amber is clearly worried about what happens to her own subjectivity if someone she considers a friend rejects that subjectivity. Kayla's rejection of compliant behavior shines a spotlight on Amber's complicity.

We can also see ISA pressure functioning through the types of media that characters within YA dystopian texts encounter. Margaret Peterson Haddix's *Among the Hidden* (1998) serves as an example. Here, Haddix gives us a picture of an America where the simple farming family of the protagonist is being driven out of that way of life by taxes and land encroachment. Luke is a forbidden third child in a population ruthlessly policed for number: each family may have no more than two children. Because of this, he must stay hidden away lest he be captured by the population police. This fictionalized RSA is precisely the type of structure that occurs again and again in works of dystopian literature. (Westerfeld calls them Special Circumstances in his *Uglies* novels; Orwell calls them the Ministry of Love in *1984*.) Because of Luke's restricted, forbidden nature, he has no official voice to protest the things being done to his family or the other "shadow children" he discovers that live in the population as well. He is not only abjected for being an adolescent, as Coats observes is a frequent condition of adolescence, but he is also further abjected because of his status as a third child (Coats 142–43).

In one particularly poignant passage, Luke is talking with Jen, another third child he has discovered living nearby. She says,

> "Well, besides passing the Population Law, the Government went on this big campaign to make women think it was something evil to get pregnant and have kids. They put posters up in all the cities with things like 'Who's the worst criminal?' under a picture of a pregnant lady and, I don't know, some tough-looking crooks. And then if you read the whole sign it'd tell you the woman was the worst of all. Another one"—Jen giggled—"it had a picture of a huge pregnant belly, with the label, 'Ladies do you want to look like this?' and women aren't allowed to go anywhere once they get pregnant.
>
> "So now, my dad told me, there are so few babies being born that the population's going to be cut in half."
>
> Luke shook his head, confused as usual. (102–3)

This particular regime has constructed even something that is constructed in our own culture as ideologically "natural" and "right," pregnancy, as a form of crime—which brings the reader immediately up against an ideological boundary. We can see in Luke's reaction that, even though he comes from this culture, the ideological construction doesn't make sense to him. Because his third child-ness has kept him from the main ISA of his culture, school, he feels as we do about the narrative world he occupies. Yet he feels powerless to do anything about his predicament because he is a third; he has no official voice. As Trites asserts, one of the very first lessons children and adolescents learn about the power they must resist, or interiorize and emulate, is that the adolescent has no official voice. Here, this silencing is doubled in that Luke is not just forbidden to speak by being an adolescent, he is a third child. One of the primary discourses in dystopian works is some form of ISA pressure—in this case, a rhetoric of "duty" to the society that attempts to restrain desire for children. By novel's end, Luke's YA status comes not just from his maturation age-wise, but also in his decision to fight against the repressive regime of the narrative. He is forced from the utopia of childhood, just as he is forced from his childhood home.

The RSA functioning within any narrative makes itself shown when a character is under bodily pressure to conform to ideological ideals. They must face some threat of being apprehended (at which point they will be bodily at the mercy of the state) all the way up through facing death at the hands of designated agents of state power. We can see examples of this in Jeanne DuPrau's *The City of Ember*.[9] In the society of this novel, children are schooled until the age of twelve.[10] At that time, they randomly draw a job out of a hat filled with all the jobs that have become vacant in the last year. Whatever job they draw, even if it has nothing to do with their interests, they are then expected to learn and perform for the rest of their working life. Lina Mayfleet hopes to get a job as a messenger, but instead receives a job in the pipeworks, the city's municipal water system. Doon Harrow receives the job as runner, but instead wants to work down in the pipeworks, because he believes that there is an answer to why the city is experiencing blackouts and food shortages. They agree to exchange jobs, and through contact with him, Lina becomes convinced that there are problems with the city and its social system, as well. Eventually, they find their way to an escape plan that the builders of Ember have had in place since its inception, but which has been lost over time.

The instructions for leaving Ember were supposed to be passed down from mayor to mayor, but have been lost and all but destroyed by the city's seventh mayor. Through happenstance, Lina comes into contact with a puzzle that, after much investigation, turns out to be those very instructions. Through the course of investigating the lower levels they find that the current mayor has a secret plan: he has been siphoning food from the storerooms, living in opulence while the rest of Ember experiences extreme shortages. When the two protagonists try to report this, city officials politely show them out the door. Eventually, though, guards come to arrest them. They have signaled (somewhat foolishly) to the authority that they no longer intend to play the game, so to speak, and remain within ISA pressure boundaries. This is when the mayor engages the RSA, in this case, the city guards, to round the children up and physically incarcerate them.

> A guard comes looking for Doon, and stops an old woman in the street not far from where Doon is trying to gather supplies to go in search of the exit from Ember:
>
> Doon could hear the guard's voice clearly: "We're looking for a boy named [Doon] Harrow."
>
> "Why?" said Nammy.
>
> "Spreading vicious rumors" was the answer. "Do you know where he is?"
>
> Nammy hesitated a moment, and then she said, "Went off to the trash heaps just a minute ago." The guard nodded curtly and beckoned to his companions. They marched away.
>
> *Spreading vicious rumors!* Doon was so stunned that he stood still as stone for a long minute. What could they possibly mean? But there was only one answer. It had to be what they'd told the assistant guard about the mayor. Why were they calling it a vicious rumor? It was the truth! He didn't understand it. (200)

The RSA representative is attempting to gain the compliance of someone he believes to identify as an "obedient citizen" by demonstrating the disobedience of the person he seeks to arrest. In a sense, this is a double hailing of the individual. The guard is not just asking "are you an obedient subject?" but also "will you help me arrest a disobedient one by your actions?" The guard is asking Nammy to disidentify with Doon, making her wish to turn him in. She, however, refuses this definition of "obedient citizen" and does not reveal that she knows where he is. The mayor goes so far to discredit Doon and Lina that guards put up posters all over the square that say, among other things, "Believe nothing they say" (205). What Lina and Doon are trying to say, though, is that there is an escape route, and that the mayor knows it. The mayor keeps people in Ember so that he can retain his secret opulent lifestyle, rather than letting the people of Ember try to escape.

Significantly, the guards fulfill their obligation as RSA by bodily enforcing ideological constructions. The guards may not find Doon, but they do find Lina:

> "[Y]ou're hurting me!" Lina said. "Don't hold so tight!"
> "Don't you tell us what to do," said the chief guard. "We'll hold you tight till we get you where you're going."
> "Where is that?" said Lina. She was so enraged at her bad luck that she almost forgot to be afraid.
> "You're going to see the mayor, missy," said the chief guard. "He'll decide what to do with you."
> "But I haven't done anything wrong!"
> "Spreading vicious rumors," said the guard. "Telling dangerous lies calculated to cause civic unrest."
> "It's not a lie!" she said. But the guard gripped her arm even more tightly and gave her a shove so she stumbled sideways.
> "No talking," he said, and they walked the rest of the way in grim silence. (214–15)

As with the posters, the important thing for the guard seems to be enforcing silence, both by discrediting the girl's words and by literally silencing her, to disidentify with someone who has been named a noncompliant subject by the power structure (in this case, the mayor). The guard has been told that Lina is lying, and so he has no desire at all to listen. Instead, his point is to apprehend her bodily. Notice, too, that when Lina is shoved by the guard, or gripped tight enough to cause pain, an adult is performing these actions on the body of a child. This is a horrifying image: an armed and uniformed guard manhandling a little girl in the name of quelling civic unrest. I believe this image is intended to push readers to the point of disgust, to make us see the RSA action as horrific overreaction. The guard is enforcing compliance bodily by what we in our rather jaded culture might call mild violence and by showing a willingness to be violent with a child, implicitly threatening worse violence.

The ISA is at work in a dystopian text when a character who is a representative of one of the ISAs (schooling system, religious system, family system) of the narrative is exerting pressure on a focalized character. RSAs are at work whenever a representative of the state charged with enforcing ideology bodily (policing system, military system, or judicial system) is exerting pressure on a focalized character. These often function in tandem, especially in a dystopian text. First, a character receives pressure to conform from the ISAs of their particular society. After a period of noncompliance, the character is then contacted by the RSAs that try to move the subject back into ideological alignment with the society using threats of (or actual) physical violence.

A Watchful Eye

As I discussed in chapter 1, another key element to the dystopian text for young adults is the ubiquitous presence of societal surveillance, as Foucault explains. Building on these ideas, Trites and Coats have demonstrated that the adolescent is always already under surveillance by his or her culture. He or she is being watched continuously for his or her moves of identification, signs of compliance with ideological constructions of abjection that are sanctioned within the culture they reside within. However, in the dystopian novel for young adults, this surveillance takes on a particularly sinister quality; the adolescent is being watched by a reified ISA or RSA representative (or representative group).

A good example of this occurs in James Dashner's novel, *The Maze Runner* (2009). Thomas, who is about sixteen, arrives at the Glade from below on the freight platform one day. The Glade, in this novel, is a society of teenaged boys who all live and work within an area bordered by walls. Just outside those walls are enormous mazes. At the point when Thomas arrives, the boys have received a new boy once a month—each boy, like Thomas, with his mind erased as to where he came from or why he is here. Each new boy is assigned to work with a particular section of the population (i.e., those who care for and slaughter animals for food, or those who care for the sick, etc.). Thomas is immediately attracted to the idea of being a runner, the ones who go out into the giant mazes every day to try to map a way out of them for the community to escape. In the end, through a long series of events, and a daring escape, the Gladers discover that they have been being tested, like rats in mazes (literally). The world they came from has been devastated by something called The Flare, and each of the Gladers has been placed in the Glade in order to test them to see who is the best and brightest. The hope is that when those one or two return, they will be able to help the world. Unfortunately, because this is only the first book in a series, the details of that other world are sparse. However, I wish to focus my examination on the life of the children in the Glade because they serve as a metaphor for ISA pressure to produce a viable subject from a child. The ISA tests them, makes them perform, and panoptically watches those performances.

The entire time he is in the Glade, Thomas encounters machines that the Gladers call Beetle Blades. These large metallic insectoids are everywhere, watching the Gladers as they go about their daily lives as well as the runners when they are in the maze. The surveillance is obviously from those who put the boys into the Glade to run the mazes, and yet the insectoids have become such a part of life that the boys don't even notice them that much. Even Thomas eventually just stops seeing them.

Thomas is accused by insinuation of many things since, from the moment he arrives in the Glade, things go much differently than they have before, especially after one of the boys, Ben, is stung by the monsters that patrol the mazes, called Grievers. When someone is stung by a Griever, we are told, they then remember what their life was like before coming to the Glade. This causes them to change and become anything from sullen to outright hostile. Ben remembers something about Thomas helping out those people who put the boys into the Glade. From this point, the other boys become suspicious that Thomas might be there to watch them—that he might be performing surveillance for the Creators. Later in the novel, Alby (one of the lead boys in the Glade) is stung. When he is first recovering, Thomas asks him if he has seen anything that might link Thomas with the Creators. As Alby tries to describe what he has seen, his face goes blank, and then he tries to strangle himself:

> "Alby..." Thomas wished he could take a peek in the boy's mind, see what he'd seen. "The Changing," he pressured, "what happened? What came back? You're not making sense."
>
> "You—," Alby started, then suddenly grabbed his own throat, making gurgly chocking sounds. His legs kicked out and he rolled onto his side, thrashing back and forth as if someone *else* were trying to strangle him. (172).

Later, after it has stopped:

> Alby looked up, eyes droopy, as if he was on the edge of slipping into a deep sleep. "I'm sorry, Newt," he whispered. "Don't know what happened. It was like... something was controlling my body. I'm sorry..."
>
> Thomas took a deep breath, sure he'd never experience something so disturbing and uncomfortable again. He hoped.
>
> "Sorries, nothin'," Newt replied. "You were trying to bloody kill yourself."
>
> "Wasn't me, I swear," Alby murmured.
>
> Newt threw his hands up. "What do you mean it wasn't you?" he asked.
>
> "I don't know... It... it wasn't me." Alby looked just as confused as Thomas felt. (174)

Not only are the boys being watched, but they are also being controlled remotely. These actions occur nowhere near a Beetle Blade, and yet Alby has been made to choke himself before he could reveal anything about what he remembers to Thomas. If Alby can have this reaction, then it is fair to believe that any of the boys can be controlled remotely, and that they are all being watched remotely, as well. Later, after Alby begins to recover, he and Thomas talk again. Thomas asks Alby once more if he saw anything:

> "Can't you tell me what you saw about me?"
> Alby shook his head. "No way, shank. Ain't gonna risk stranglin' myself again. Might be something they got in our brains to control us—just like the memory wipe." (198)

The Creators' behavior modification tool has worked—Alby has no intention of revealing too much more about what he has seen to Thomas for fear of being punished by those who are invisibly watching for signs of transgression.

Toward the end of the novel, Thomas finally allows himself to be stung by a Griever in order to recover his own memories. When he does, he reveals them to the rest of the Gladers: "The Creators are testing us. The Maze was never meant to be solved. It's all been a trial. They want the winners—or survivors—to do something important" (302). Then he continues after few more exchanges and says, "Supposedly, we're really smart and they're studying every move we make, analyzing us. Seeing who'd give up and who wouldn't. Seeing who'd survive it all. No wonder we have so many beetle blade spies running around this place. Plus some of us had things ... altered in our brains" (303). The boys are literally being tested like lab rats and observed for their reactions. Though this is an intentionally hyperbolic case, this mirrors the ways that we as a culture test adolescents and watch them for their reactions. Here, metaphorically, is both the surveillance by and the abjection of the social body that Trites and Coats describe.[11]

In the end, after the Gladers fight through and manage to make it to the outside world, they come face to face with the Creators, who appear to be still testing them and observing their responses. In the end of the novel, a group of people break in and take the Gladers who have made it through out of the facility they emerged in. This happens before more answers can be found, but again—for now, the important part of the narrative (indeed, the bulk of it, page-wise) is about the society of the Glade that functions knowing full well that it is being watched. These adolescents are constantly under the eye of unseen forces, watching their moves of identification and actions based on those moves.

Another example of this occurs in Neal Shusterman's novel *Unwind* (2007), in which three adolescents are bound to be unwound. The primary focalizer of the novel is Connor Lassiter, sixteen, who comes from what we might call a suburban family; he has a father, a mother, and a little brother. Risa, fifteen years old, is an aspiring pianist from Ohio State Home 23. We also meet Lev Calder, thirteen, and the youngest of ten in his family, who is a Tithe. Tithes are children who are given up to be unwound as a religious obligation. In fact, being a Tithe helps him redefine himself. Once he is saved from unwinding by Connor, he sees it as being kidnapped by a "dirty Unwind" (31).

In the society of the novel, to be unwound means to be aborted retroactively. Within the narrative, the concept is that a child between the ages of thirteen and seventeen may be unwound, in which case all of their body parts are removed from them to be given to those who need organ/limb donations.[12] Within the novel, we are told, a second civil war has occurred. This one was between the Life Army, the Choice Brigade, and the United States Army, sent in to try to keep the two warring factions peaceful (223). After the war is brought to a close, the process of neurografting is perfected, which allows every part of a person to be used for transplants. The Bill of Life comes from this conflict, allowing a pregnancy to be terminated retroactively (223–24). Of course, this is thinly disguised social criticism. In essence, Shusterman is proposing, like Solomon, that the disputed child be divided in two, just with technology and medicine instead of an axe. Nonetheless, the debate is played out in fascinating and instructive ways.

The three adolescents "kick AWOL" (meaning that they either choose to not report for unwinding and escape, or in the case of Lev, are kidnapped and prevented from doing so) and then go into an underground railroad of those willing to help unwinds escape. The three eventually end up in the Admiral's airplane graveyard. This is especially apt, in that airplane graveyards are real places where airplanes are sent to sit when they are taken from service; if a plane that is currently in service requires a part, the airplane graveyard is scoured for the replacement piece. It is a powerful recycling concept, and a somewhat subtle metaphor for the unwinding process, itself. Eventually, Connor and Risa are captured and nearly unwound, eventually being rescued by a group of Clappers Lev has joined. Clappers are suicide terrorists or freedom fighters, whichever side of the debate you may be on, who flood their bodies with explosives so that they can blow themselves up with the slightest impact, such as clapping their hands together. In the end, the Clappers destroy the unwinding center. Coupled with the issue of the young age of the only attacker left alive, Lev, the destruction brings attention to ethical issues of retroactively "aborting" teenagers, and the reader is left somewhat hopeful that the society of the novel will regain their sanity and end this horrific process.

In an interesting reversal, Shusterman shows that not only are the children being watched in their society (with unwinding as the consequence of failure to conform to sanctioned subjectivity), but also even in the airplane graveyard where the AWOLs find shelter, there is still always surveillance: "The Admiral never attends, but there are video feeds from the meeting canopy, just as there are feeds all over the yard, so everyone knows he's watching. Whether or not every camera is constantly monitored, no one knows, but the potential for being seen is always there" (204–5). This is the classic definition of panopticism. Even if no one is watching, the children feel as if someone always might be, and they internalize the behavior that they are expected to exhibit.

Perhaps the most shocking incident of panopticism within Shusterman's novel occurs relatively close to the end of the novel. While in the unwinding center, Risa notices that several of the boys that are playing basketball (while waiting to be unwound) are being watched:

> Exercise seems to be a principle component of the Unwind's day. At first she assumed the various activities were designed to keep the Unwinds occupied until their number came up. Then, as she passed a basketball game on the way to the welcome center, she noticed a totem pole by the court. In the eyes of each of the five totems were cameras. Ten players, ten cameras. It meant that someone, somewhere, was studying each of the Unwinds in that game, taking notes on the eye-hand coordination, gauging the strengths of various muscle groups. Risa had quickly realized that the basketball game wasn't to keep the Unwinds entertained, but to help put cash value on their parts. (268)

The realization is quite shocking. The intrusive nature of the panoptic devices into an area of play for children is already appalling, but when the reader considers that the purpose here is not merely to watch them for their behavior (as disciplined bodies), but also to size up their bodies for market value, this seems deplorable. Here is a comment on the commodity fetishism of the adolescent body that we see in our own contemporary culture taken to extremes. One can imagine that, should an adolescent's behavior become violent during one of these games, the fight wouldn't just be broken up in the name of discipline, but also in the name of protecting the merchandise.

Not Necessarily SF

Even someone as well read on the subject of science fiction as Robert Scholes has made the mistake of classifying this type of dystopian literature as science fiction. In his book *Structural Fabulation*, he says: "Some of the most powerful and cognitively useful works of SF have been projections into the near future, like Orwell's *1984*, Zamyatin's *We*, and Anthony Burgess's *Clockwork Orange* and *The Wanting Seed*" (71). All of these works fall squarely into the category of dystopian literature. Scholes's definition of them as works that occur in the "near future" marks them as being science fiction for him. Even Fredric Jameson believes that dystopian literature is a subcategory of science fiction.[13]

However, with the schema that I am plotting here, we can begin to see that dystopian literature for young people is neither always already nor only science fiction. As I will show via a reading of Cormier's *The Chocolate War* and Todd Strasser's *The Wave* (1974 and 1981, respectively), issues of surveillance and social pressure can be seen in texts that do not necessarily take place in a future setting at all. In some ways, this may seem confusing, given my stance that the adjective "dystopian" does not always mark a text as dystopian literature, but more often as merely a world that has fallen into disrepair after some form of disaster. However, what I will show is that it is important to recognize these texts as doing separate work—which is to say, they have different use values. There are a number of texts that routinely get classified as dystopian by critics, such as the postapocalyptic story.[14] I strongly believe that types of narratives such as the post-disaster story and the modification of that, the zombie narrative, are very different. Though some stories involve an element of both, a popular way to construct a dystopian narrative is to show the results of postapocalyptic rebuilding.[15] The potential for these rebuilt societies to go wrong is a powerful draw for the dystopian author. However, the point of the story differs from the goal of postapocalyptic narratives. I determine the difference by asking these questions: Is the story set during the reign of a totalitarian regime in order to highlight the ways that we are constructed socially? Or is it merely a decayed urban setting with the narrative concerned with other ideological issues?[16]

This slippage occurs most often because the term "dystopia" is being used connotatively rather than denotatively. Quite often, the term "dystopian" is used when what the critic really means is dystopic. "Dystopian" literature delineates a narrative about totalitarian regimes and the subjectivities of its citizens, while "dystopic" literature is a more generalized term that describes a decayed urban sprawl setting. For instance, there are many types of fictional societies that we may, for one reason or another, deem dystopic. This does not mean, however, that they are actually dystopian narratives. For example, postapocalyptic narratives are often called dystopic simply because they are filled with a sense of urban decay. However, they are more often than not focused on completely different ideological issues. This is where a great deal of confusion comes in for readers, I believe. Ostry and Hintz say that the genre of the post-disaster story deserves its own study (5), and I agree.

Dystopian writing does not fit easily into the category of science fiction, although it is easily perceived as slipping into other literary categories, such as postapocalyptic literature. But use value helps clarify the social purpose of these differing types of novels. We can see an important example of a non-science-fiction dystopian novel in Todd Strasser's *The Wave*. The novel is based on the 1969 Palo Alto incident at Gordon High School, when students formed a community inside the student body called The Wave. This community eventually became totalitarian, taking the already dystopian landscape of the contemporary American high school and mapping yet another level of surveillance and power onto it. The novel follows a number of students, as well as the teacher responsible for beginning the movement, Ben Ross. The primary focalizer, though, is Laurie Sanders, a student very interested in journalism. Ross initially begins the community by attempting to create more discipline in his classroom. When that discipline begins to have a kind of quantifiable result in the categories of student attendance and grades, some of the students take on the community and spread it further than Ross's classroom. The main student who spreads The Wave outside Ross's classroom is David Collins, the running back for the football team, and Laurie's boyfriend. We can see the effect that this attempted-utopian community has when, near the end of the novel, Laurie (who has been more and more alarmed by the ways that The Wave community has changed high school society around her) confronts David:

> "Don't you see," Laurie said, mistaking his hesitation for a glimmer of doubt. "You're so idealistic, David. You're so intent on creating some kind of utopian Wave society full of equal people and great football teams that you don't see it at all. It can't happen, David. There will always be a few people who won't want to join. They have the right not to join."
>
> David squinted at his girlfriend. "You know," he said, "you're just against this thing because you're not special anymore. Because you're not the best and most popular student in the class now." (88)

On some level, David has genuinely wanted to make a utopian society. At one point he even remarks that he doesn't understand why everyone does not want to join. Eventually, his belief and trust in the Wave concept leads him to a confrontation with his girlfriend. One small part of her response demonstrates just how this maps dystopia onto the high school experience. She feels things have gone so far that she actually has to point out to David that people have the right to not join The Wave if they so choose. He does not agree, and he takes upon himself the full authority of an ISA in that his immediate response to her is not to engage with her ideas, but instead to use social pressure. He points out that he believes her only reason for rejecting The Wave community is that to enter into it would remove her from her former position of power. We can extrapolate from this belief that those who don't want to join have similar reasons for rejecting the community, such as ego response (characters believing that they are "too good" to join), rather than genuine critical rejection. In this one passage, we can also see the characteristic of totalitarian society that is so heartbreaking: at some point, there has been a utopian ideal that could never work when put into a living, breathing society, and a charismatic leader who has somewhere along the way forgotten that society thrives when it is heterogeneous. In this way, David stands in for Castro, for Mao, for Jim Jones, for Stalin, for Hitler.

Robert Cormier's *The Chocolate War* also shows that dystopian works are not necessarily science fiction. In this novel, the main character is Jerry Renault, a fourteen-year-old whose mother died just a bit before the novel begins. He is a freshman at a Catholic private school called Trinity. Every year, this school has a fund-raising activity, and the students are asked to garner funds for the school by selling boxes of chocolate. The school is run not only by its administration, though, but also by an unauthorized gang of boys called The Vigils. As the novel begins, Brother Leon has had to take temporary control of the school and has high hopes that he might become permanent headmaster if he can get the boys to sell twice the normal amount of chocolate this year while he is in charge. Archie, though, a boy who leads The Vigils, is power hungry as well. So when Brother Leon approaches Archie to ask for his help motivating the student body to sell that amount of chocolate, Archie decides that he will demonstrate his power by forcing one student to refuse to sell, allowing Archie to step in, solve the problem, and thereby gain much more power for The Vigils. Archie chooses to put pressure on Jerry to not sell the chocolate, a plan that backfires because Jerry continues to refuse to sell the chocolate even after The Vigils order him to resume his sales. Eventually this conflict escalates and Jerry is marked as *homo sacer* by the community of the school, thanks to ISA pressure and eventually bodily attack. He is perhaps destroyed, depending on the interpretation of the ending that a reader has, by the RSA. The community feels so strongly about his alienation that he is no longer protected—the community feels they may do with him whatever they wish. In this novel, we can clearly see The Vigils acting as the RSA arm of the ISAs that function within the school's culture. The narrator says of The Vigils:

> No one was allowed to breathe a word about The Vigils. Officially, The Vigils did not exist. How could a school condone an organization like

The Vigils? The schools allowed it to function by ignoring it completely, pretending it wasn't there ... The Vigils kept things under control. Without The Vigils, Trinity might have been torn apart like other schools had been by demonstrations, protests, all that crap. (27)

Only the threat of action by The Vigils keeps the unrest of the Vietnam War and the counterculture movement from influencing students at Trinity. They act as an RSA within the school in this way: they bodily enforce ideological conformity. Subjects identify with the position "student" as equaling obedient and patriotic, or they risk bodily harm. The administration, another RSA branch within the community of the school, allows this to occur, making The Vigils an unacknowledged though still sanctioned "secret" policing force.

Brother Leon, knowing of Archie's connection to The Vigils, puts pressure on him to help get students motivated, to use the word perversely, to sell. The quota is doubled this particular year, with each boy having to sell at least fifty boxes of chocolates. Of course, as is often the case with RSAs, Archie begins to think of The Vigils as beyond the control of the ISA (in this case, represented by Brother Leon). Even before this exchange, Archie begins to plot against Brother Leon by manipulating Jerry to refuse to sell. Brother Leon can clearly be seen defining subjectivity in response to Jerry's refusal, here:

> "Let me get this straight, Renault," Brother Leon said and his voice brought the room under his command again. "I called your name. Your response could have been either *yes* or *no*. *Yes* means that like every other student in this school you agree to sell a certain amount of chocolates, in this cases fifty boxes. *No*—and let me point out that the sale is strictly voluntary, Trinity forces no one to participate against his wishes, this is the great glory of Trinity—*no* means you don't wish to sell the chocolates, that you refuse to participate." (84)

Obviously, participation is in fact not voluntary. This is ISA pressure in the extreme. Jerry is forced by The Vigils to say no, and in response

Brother Leon defines him publicly as someone who wishes to reject the culture around him. All the rest of the boys in the class agree to sell the chocolates, making Jerry's task all the more difficult. Rather than merely refusing the commercialism of the school, Jerry is now seen as violating social contract. At the end of the exchange, Brother Leon says, "You may pick up your chocolates in gym, gentlemen, [...] Those of you who are true sons of Trinity, that is. I pity anyone who is not" (86). Instead of just being seen as refusing the commercialist endeavor of the school, Brother Leon defines a clear boundary: the "us" who is willing to sell chocolates and therefore worthy of being a part of society, and a "them," which consists only of Jerry. This kind of public pressure leads up to another incident, after Jerry has continued to refuse to sell the chocolates, when a fellow student even asks Brother Leon to ask Jerry in class why he isn't selling. This will require Jerry to announce in a public space his intention and reasoning. Here is the public confession, the ISA taking it upon itself to force a member of society to explain him or herself:

> Brother Leon's face was guarded. "Why do you want to know?" he asked.
> "I figure it's my right to know. The right of everybody to know." He looked around for support. Somebody called out "Right on." Darcy said, "Everybody else is doing their part, why isn't Renault?"
> "Would you care to answer that, Renault?" the teacher said, the moist eyes flashing, the malice unmistakable.
> "It's a free country," he said, words which touched off a ripple of laughter. Someone snickered. Brother Leon looked positively joyous and Goober felt nauseous.
> "I'm afraid you'll have to be more original than that, Renault," Brother Leon said, playing to his audience, as usual....
> ..."Did you say this sale was voluntary, Brother Leon?" Jerry asked.
> "Yes," the teacher said, hanging back as if he were trying to fade into the background, letting Jerry betray himself with his own words.
> "Then I don't feel that I have to sell the chocolates."

A ripple of resentment across the classroom.
"You think you're better than we are?" Darcy shot out. (204–5)

ISA pressure to conform is at work here; Jerry is being asked to share his sense of his subjectivity boldface, on record, to the community. In a Foucauldian sense, he is being asked to confess. Jerry's refusal to sell the chocolates goes from being a personal matter to being a threat to the entire community. They believe that his refusal highlights their complicity in a negative way. Eventually, Jerry is moved beyond the position of scapegoat into the position of *homo sacer*. His continued refusal to join the community's endeavor to sell chocolate marks him as beyond their contempt. As Agamben defines it, Jerry's community no longer feels his life is sacred, and may therefore destroy him in any way they choose. It is decided that there will be a fight between Jerry and the school bully, Janza. Because Janza is so much more skilled at fighting, randomly drawn raffle tickets determine who gets to do what to whom. In the end, though, the raffle is fixed by Archie so that Jerry cannot win, and Jerry receives a horrific beating. He is at least symbolically (and perhaps physically, depending on the function of that first sentence of the novel) murdered by novel's end. His refusal to be placed back into the ISA cycle by the RSA (The Vigils) costs him his life (at least socially, and perhaps physically). One cannot help but be reminded of Orwell's Winston Smith.

The Giver

I would argue that any examination of dystopian literature for young adults would be incomplete without looking at Lois Lowry's *The Giver*. Though coming along late in 1993, Lowry's novel is every bit as foundational to the concept of dystopian writing for young adults as Orwell's *1984* is to the study of adult dystopian literature. Because of its iconic nature, I have left the novel to its own section in order to examine it in some depth as a type of case study.

The novel follows the life of Jonas Eleven Nineteen, an eleven-year-old who is about to undergo the ceremony that will move him into a time of adulthood by the standards of the society that he lives within (at which point he will simply be Jonas without the numeric designation). Jonas has a special gift—a type of telepathy that allows him to receive and distribute memory by touch. Because of this he is apprenticed to the community's Giver, the person who is the living receptacle of memories of how things were "before." It is through his reception of those memories that Jonas begins to see the idyllic utopia he lives within for the repressive regime that it is. He eventually escapes from the community and, as in Cormier's *The Chocolate War*, Lowry's ending is somewhat ambiguous—it is entirely possible that Jonas makes it to another community that is not a repressive dystopia, or he may have died attempting to find some place outside of conformist ideology.[17]

One of the primary things I wish to discuss in terms of the novel is the sense of order as produced by rules. Jonas spends quite a bit of time thinking about rules. We can see ISA pressure in Jonas's reactions to others, especially within a brief passage in which Jonas is thinking about his interactions with Pierre Eleven Twenty, a boy that Jonas says he

> ... didn't like very much. Pierre was very serious, not much fun, and a worrier and a tattletale, too. "Have you checked the rules, Jonas?" Pierre was always whispering solemnly. "I'm not sure that's within the rules." Usually it was some foolish thing that no one cared about—opening his tunic if it was a day with a breeze; taking a brief try on a friend's bicycle, just to experience the different feel of it. (51)

Jonas values experience and has an internal sense of a gradation of rules. On a few occasions, he reacts himself to infractions, however:

> Fritz was a very awkward child who had been summoned for chastisement again and again. His transgressions were small ones, always: shoes

on the wrong feet, schoolwork misplaced, failure to study adequately for a quiz. But each such error reflected negatively on his parents' guidance and infringed on the community's sense of order and success. (45)

Jonas is always thinking about rules and their gradations. These passages illustrate, however, that this seeming utopia where everyone's needs are met is an extremely strict sort of community. These are children, and yet we're told that they are routinely punished for very minor offenses, as though the actions were affronts to the community's well-being. Consider that Asher, a boy who is continuously in trouble for offenses that we would consider just being awkward, has to deliver something called a "standard apology phrase" for being late to class. Within that phrase, he has to mention that he is sorry for "inconveniencing my learning community" (3). In all of these cases we can see that there is ISA pressure at work—the community requires even children to acknowledge their place in it. They must reaffirm their attachment with each chastisement.

Jonas is fascinated when his father reveals that he has broken a rule: Jonas's father went to find out the name of an infant that he is caring for. This is something none of the nursery workers are supposed to do. Jonas is taken aback, "He was fascinated. It didn't seem a terribly important rule, but the fact that his father had broken a rule at all awed him" (12). Jonas has a sense of gradation of rules, something that no one else in the community seems to have (save Jonas's father).

His fascination with the minor rules that govern daily behavior is a precursor to his receiving the list of new rules about being the Receiver of Memory. Almost all of them involve retractions of the rules he has worked very hard to gain mastery of over time. For instance, rule number 3 of the Receiver directly states that Jonas may now lie (68). Lowry tells us immediately after showing us this list of the new rules for Jonas, "Jonas was stunned. What would happen to his friendships? His mindless hours playing ball, or riding his bike along the river?" (69). His first thoughts are not those of exaltation—

instead, he worries about his community connections once the rules that bind him to that community are eased. The phrases are all standing in for the romantic conception of childhood, metonymically, as a carefree time. In essence, Jonas is being evicted from this concept of childhood, which he had come to have. His "carefree" time is over. Like Luke from Haddix's novel, Jonas's passage out of the community works as a passage from utopia to dystopia. We might map over this a passage from childhood to adolescence, except that the seemingly utopian community is actually a dystopian one from the outset. Once the Giver makes Jonas witness his own father murdering a baby, the smaller twin of the two in that generation deemed too small to be viable for the community, he sees that the idyllic community he lives in is only so on the surface. It is a shallow utopia. This scene is made all the more chilling by his father's soothing words to the infant (148–49). This is the impetus that causes Jonas to finally decide to leave the community.

Teaching the Future

Dystopian texts for young adults are a distinct entity from science fiction for adolescents. The two genres do different work. Hintz and Ostry believe this is true, as well. They say, "exposure to these types of texts can lead young readers to see inequality in their own communities and countries, and even lead them into a finer understanding of how the industrialized world exploits developing nations" (8). This is why it is essential that we as critics, librarians, and instructors recognize the use value of these genres. If our goals as critics of children's literature are to provide an advocacy for children and young adults, then we must recognize how important it is for us to get these texts into the hands of those who need them most. By understanding the difference between science fiction for adolescents and dystopian literature for young adults, we can more effectively use these texts to help them.

In the next chapter we will explore exactly how we can go about using these texts in classrooms. Specifically, I will explore how I used Lowry's *The Giver* and Orwell's *1984* with a group of late adolescents (recognizing that in twenty-first-century American culture, adolescence has telescoped to include those who are in their early twenties) in a course exploring the differences between science fiction and dystopian literature.

4

"Teaching the Fantastic": Using Science Fiction and Dystopian Texts in the Classroom

In this chapter, I will examine pedagogical statements about science fiction and dystopia in the classroom.[1] I will then briefly examine some of the theoretical underpinnings of my own thoughts on pedagogy and how they relate to teaching science fiction and/or dystopian literature in the classroom space. Finally, I will discuss some of the significant pedagogical issues that occurred during my own teaching of a course designed to help undergraduate non-English majors explore the differences between these two genres.

I should also note that, in this chapter, I am relying on theorists who write about teaching science fiction in elementary school, middle/high school, or college. While I recognize that there are many differences in the concerns of instructors at these three levels, I do this because of (1) the relative rarity of SF pedagogy theory, and (2) the shared concerns the theory demonstrates, regardless of grade level.

A History of (Teaching) the Future

A historical overview of how science fiction (and dystopian lit) came into the classroom space, as well as the issues involved, will help to contextualize my pedagogical discussion. Here, I will provide a brief sketch of the history of science fiction instruction. Then I will explore some of the controversies that arose from the explosion of science fiction teaching.

By the 1950s (as explored in chapter 2), science fiction had entered its Golden Age. Dystopian literature (as explored in chapter 3) was then in its late infancy, just about to produce its major works. John Rodden illustrates what I mean when he says that "although a 1955 secondary school survey showed that *1984* (1949) was one of thirty novels most commonly read by college-bound seniors, it was not widely taught in schools until the early 1960s" (509).[2] Rodden goes on to point out that:

> In a 1969 survey, university-bound British and American students ranked *1984* among their most "personally significant" books. British students also listed Orwell in fourth position as "the author who had greatest influence on them." A 1971 survey among A-level students found Orwell, after Lawrence, the most popular "serious" author—with Hardy third, and Shakespeare fourth. (510)[3]

This movement of Orwell's novel from outside the classroom to the classroom canon is important because this is a text that is very often thought of as science fiction. Moreover, it was popular with students. Of course, Orwell's *1984* is only one of the many texts that would show this trend, which was not only in texts moving into the classroom. Courses on the subject continuously rose in number, as well. Science fiction author and pedagogy theorist Jack Williamson says that "by 1974, when I gave up on the project because it had grown out of hand, I had found some 500 courses offered at the college level in the United States and Canada" (10). Patrick Parrinder says,

As far as I know, the first college SF course was taught by Sam Moskowitz at the City College of New York in 1953. The first to have any impact in educational circles was Mark R. Hillegas' course which began in Colgate in 1962. Five years later, Hillegas, who was now at Southern Illinois University, published an article reflecting somewhat dispiritedly on his experiences as an SF teacher ... Hillegas reported growing opposition from his faculty colleagues. (131)

There was a great deal of attention paid to theorizing pedagogies of science fiction by 1980, with two of the major texts on the subject being published that year.[4] This may be due to the discussion that had just happened at the MLA in December 1978.[5] There was a great deal of debate at the time as to whether or not science fiction "belonged" in a classroom setting from more traditional literature camps, and questions also arose about the qualifications of teachers to teach science fiction from those who consumed and produced the genre.

James Gunn, science fiction author, one of the pioneers of science fiction pedagogy and director of the Gunn Center for Study of Science Fiction at University of Kansas, speaks of a "ghetto," an "us-against-them" attitude in science fiction fandom that existed in 1980, pitting science fiction readers against academics. He says he feels it was this divide that has given science fiction fandom its strength and science fiction writers their feelings of brotherhood; this feeling created a suspicion about the teaching of science fiction in a classroom setting (*Inside* 67). Along those lines, Carolyn Wendell reminds us that "some have protested that English teachers could not possibly know enough about science to teach science fiction" (105). As for the students, Patrick Parrinder suggests that "students who enroll in an SF course do not necessarily know much about the genre. Many, in fact, feel quite ignorant about it, despite its apparent accessibility to them" (141). Gunn says he feels that, "in addition, some teachers may feel unqualified to teach science fiction as a genre, or prefer to use sf for other purposes, or believe that sf should be read and evaluated according to the same criteria as any other literature and thus needs no special instruction" ("Teaching" 377). Speaking of an experience he had watching a large group of people reading science fiction on a ferry, Anderson says, "I understood, once again, how the generalizations we make about literature can block off more communication between students and teachers than they open up" (203). Such comments as this demonstrate that the concept of teaching science fiction in its own right, instead of engaging with its use value to teach other concepts, is relatively new.

The predominant questions that drive science fiction pedagogy center on how the genre is to be used and how well the instructor has been trained to teach the subject. What qualifies a teacher to teach science fiction is a justified question (Gunn, *Inside* 68). Is the teacher teaching the genre as a means to an end, pedagogically, or does the instructor inherently love the genre? Of course, this is a troubling assertion: instructors don't teach only what they "love," and the idea of an instructor bringing the genre he or she loves most into the classroom could be problematic, as Gunn—a science fiction author, reader and critic—demonstrates. What is the instructor using the genre for, and what are his or her qualifications to teach the genre? These are the predominant issues that drove science fiction pedagogy early on.[6] Both Jack Williamson and James Gunn are advocates for SF in the classroom. Williamson believes that "the most successful teachers are motivated, I think, by a sense that science fiction has a special relevance to life in our transitional times" (15). James Gunn points out that "we all use SF for our own purposes, authors, fans, editors, the lot, and I didn't see why teachers and scholars should be excluded" (*Inside* 157). I appreciate Gunn's point of view a great deal: I think there is much to be gained in bringing these texts into the classroom space. To reject such a move based on a sense of privileged usage would deny students a myriad of opportunities that these texts can provide.

A Speculative Pedagogy

SF pedagogical theorists seem to imply that science fiction pedagogy falls into one of two categories: either we teach SF as a tool to help students learn science (a category in which I include political science, linguistics, etc.), or we teach it because it fosters critical thought.[7] Those who use science fiction to teach other concepts and those who teach it as a literature in its own right provide different insights into the pedagogy of English Studies. Instructors who advocate using science fiction to teach other concepts tend to want to use it for its use value in teaching the sciences. They often believe that speculation about science can be used as a "teachable moment," lending a relevance to the sometimes-abstract nature of science education, which could be particularly useful for college-level writing across the curriculum courses or in the K–12 classroom. For example, astronomer Carl Sagan says that he thinks science fiction should be in the classroom, but that "courses in which there is no attempt to extend the science-fiction plot line to encompass the appropriate science miss a great educational opportunity" (7). Barry Longyear, speaking about using science fiction in the elementary school setting, says that "the 'science' in the story can then be picked out and discussed. Not only will this cast the students' usual text material in a new light, it will also help to nurture that 'what if' quality necessary to the student scientist" (80). Using science fiction to teach the concept of evolution, Andrea Bixler says:[8]

> Sci fi stories and films can be used in a variety of ways in the classroom. Teachers may assign reading to be done outside of class, then use small-group or general classroom discussion to draw out all the flaws in the author's evolutionary scenarios. Alternatively, discussion can focus on what aspects of the environment could lead to the adaptations of the organisms, or even whether the species' characteristics are adaptations. (337)

In other words, in the approach that advocates for using science fiction as a means to lend relevance to scientific concepts, the genre itself is not the point: science education is. However, this approach poses significant difficulties to the instructor because science fiction, no matter what the age range of the intended audience, is inherently an interdisciplinary genre.

There are those instructors, though, who are attempting to use science fiction texts in order to do important work in the classroom that does not center solely on the genre itself, but that also does not fit neatly into the above category. For example, Jane Donawerth feels that the science-fiction-for-science-instruction approach might help encourage female students to enter science fields. She says:

> Teaching science fiction by women, then, offers a counterbalance to these causes of girls' lack of interest in science: worlds in which men and women participate equally in scientific discovery; role models in the portrayals of women scientists; and a mode of arousing interest in science, through literature, that is traditionally more congenial to female students. It is important, then, for teachers to encourage students to discuss the careers of the characters and to explore the kinds of science that the writer makes central to the novel. (40)

She makes an important point here that science fiction might be one of the few literatures that not only concerns itself with science, but that also often shows women engaged in that enterprise—at least in the case of science fiction that has come since the 1970s. She does point out, though, that some selection on the part of the instructor may be necessary, and for precisely that reason. She says that

> To overcome [the implication that only male writers can achieve quality], we can ask students to read paired stories by a man and a woman and then to try their own hands at writing science fiction; or we can ask students, after reading a utopia, to write one utopia for women and one for men, afterwards discussing the differences as results of either gender

stereotyping, or of an understanding of the different experiences of men and women in our culture. (41)

Thus, although the science and women scientists are the central point of Donawerth's pedagogical use of science fiction, she also has gender ideology in mind as an explorative topic.

We might also include in this category those instructors who use science fiction texts as means to begin discussion. This was the case with Erland Anderson's composition course. Anderson intended to use science fiction in a composition class to generate discussion on composing. He says, though, that the students resisted, often being more interested in discussing the prose stylistics, or in discussing empirical world events that related to the plot. He says:

> Out of frustration more than conviction, I decided to let the class do what they wanted to do with the literature. If they wanted to speculate about the robots of the future without making clear references to the text, I let them. If they wanted to compare a scene in *Stranger in a Strange Land* with the Watergate conspiracy, I let them. If they wanted to take a statement on euthanasia in *Canticle for Leibowitz* out of context in order to expound on their own sense of the problem in hospitals today, I let them. Soon most of them discovered that their reading related to almost every aspect of their lives, including some of their most personal religious and philosophic beliefs. The connections were there even though they were often extremely tenuous. (204)

Anderson's discovery parallels my own argument: science fiction and dystopian literature are topical. The way "in to" the text for many students is through the allegorical relations they pose to the world we as readers live in. Anderson goes on to note that, "In general, I suspended my own critical judgments and let the students in the class confront each other on the issues which they raised. For a while, I became an instigator rather than a teacher; I prodded the class with questions rather than giving my own answers. It became my policy to withhold my interpretation and to let the students carry their own discussions" (205). Eventually, Anderson observed that he could use science fiction to make connections to other literatures, and if he empowered students to answer each other's questions, "they came to me for interpretative answers when they were ready instead of listening to me first and then trying to 'please' me with the 'right' answers in their papers" (205). In the end, Anderson discovered that science fiction works best to create spaces for conversations on politics or history, but perhaps does not work as well for conversations on composition. Echoing other SF pedagogical theorists, he says, "The class convinced me that SF works well as a stimulus for topics which students want to write about. Part of the reason it works so well in this respect is that it is a literature that belongs to the students first and to the teachers second" (206). I'm not sure I agree with this, because it assumes that the instructor has no contact with science fiction while students have a great deal. He assumes that because this is a genre that (at least at the time) is popular, and often not taught in classrooms, that students will have had more contact with science fiction than instructors. Anderson (like Donawerth) implies, though, that when an instructor brings these texts into the classroom, then the most significant aspect of science fiction (and dystopian literature, because he doesn't make that distinction, though I do) is its use value to instructors.

Katie Rybakova and Rikki Roccanti suggest that we might use YA texts as bridges to the canon. "Although literary critics and educators debate the pros and cons of classical and contemporary texts, we believe that these two categories of texts are most powerful when they are connected rather than when they are pitted against one another" (31). They point out that by using both simultaneously, students can be shown that reading for pleasure and analytical reading are not antithetical (34). So, for instance, they suggest pairing a YA novel with a more canonical one based on connecting elements/themes, using the more approachable text as a scaffold to reach the more challenging. Imagine using Shusterman's *Unwind* as a way to help students into *Fahrenheit 451*.

> Teaching literature in the secondary classroom does not have to be a debate about whether including YAL will detract from a focus on canonical text. Rather than arguing that one type of text is better than the other, we have tried to show how connecting YAL to the canon can serve as a reading ladder for students which blends the benefits of both types of texts with the ultimate goal of developing literacy. (Rybakova and Roccanti, 43)

Their suggestion may be one way of bringing YA SF and/or YA dystopian texts out of the marginalized place they have been into mainstream lesson plans.

George McKay suggests that we can use the genre of dystopian writing to help students to do what he calls "self-reading." He is among those who theorize science fiction for its use value within English Studies. He says:

> This is one of the things I am interested in here: what I term (after autobiography theory's coining of the term self-writing) *self-reading*. I look at how the conjunction of text and self, where the one contributes to the construction of the other, is achieved through *reading* a text rather than writing one [. . .] There is a socio-critical impulse at work. [. . .] They are textual critiques of (intra-textual) societies embedded in textual critiques of (extra-textual) societies. (303)

His concept of a parallel moment of "self-reading" that occurs for both focalizer and reader simultaneously allows the reader to see what critical intervention into ideology might look like. Thus, McKay upholds the idea that these texts provide a discourse that encourages self-examination.

Because of their inherently critical orientation toward culture, science fiction and dystopian literature are ideal texts for stimulating self-reflexive examination in a classroom. Readers cannot help but call their ideological constructions and dispositions toward the other into question when the text's entire purpose is to inveigle them to do so. Such literature, it seems to me, must also be paired with a pedagogy that allows for such critical reflection. Dave Samuelson says of his own pedagogy for science fiction courses:

> I try to make sure that my students have access to what I know and what their classmates know about science and technology, our industrial (or post-industrial) age, literature in general, and science fiction in particular. I lecture occasionally. I ask them to read the historical and theoretical introductions to science fiction from my *Visions of Tomorrow*. I point them toward other relevant background materials, and I compile and distribute a Student Directory with names, addresses, phone numbers, academic majors and personal interests in SF. Breaking down artificial classroom barriers, I also try to get them to share ideas in class discussion and through reading each other's journals, making learning a more cooperative and less competitive activity. I try to take advantage of the whole disparity in academic backgrounds students bring to an SF class, enabling all students to feel of value, contributing what they know, and learn from their peers (not just from me). Through this cross-talk, I hope by the end of the course that they are all acquainted with some idea of literature, literary standards, and critical tools, with arguments for the legitimacy of popular culture and commercial literature, with respect for science and technology, and with a healthy skepticism about conventional social attitudes. (195)

Samuelson does not explicitly state it, but he implies that he is creating community. He is working with the shared discourses and knowledges that come from the community of fans who appreciate science fiction and integrating those discourses into the classroom's social architecture. Samuelson says that "a high compliment I once received was that I didn't seem like the teacher, but more like 'the best prepared student in class'" (196). This is an important thing to note in teaching both science fiction as well as dystopian literature, no matter what the age group of the readership: they are literatures that can frustrate the more traditional top-down power structures of the classroom. As Parrinder has said, "Teaching SF, it may be added, is different from teaching the more self-contained literary modes (such as modern poetry) in that it is impossible, as well as undesirable, to maintain the illusion there is one kind of knowledge involved, which the teacher has access to and the students, initially, do not" (137). Certain parts of education regarding these literatures must be put into place by the instructor (vocabulary terms, for instance), but overall I agree with Samuelson and Parrinder on this point. When used for their social criticism (and not for their technological-predictive aspect), these literatures can help to create not only self-reflexive moments of examination for the student, but they can also knock down some of the power boundaries that exist within the classroom. Studying science fiction and dystopian literatures can create a learning community within the classroom space.

Dennis Livingston emphasizes the critical aspects of the literature by asking students to engage in their own thought experiments. He says that in his courses, which he calls science fiction but which are much more dystopian oriented, students

> are to select a particular present or near-future problem/opportunity in public policy, analyze possible solutions to it offered in relevant SF stories and films, and compare these SF solutions to any speculation and proposals being offered in nonfiction. There is obviously no lack of possible topics here: subjects in which SF has a lot to say include overpopulations, pollution, nuclear war, cybernation and unemployment, anomie in a mass society, crime, energy/resource depletion, etc. In this way, students are encouraged to begin to exercise their own rights as participants in shaping real-time futures for our society. (202)

He asks the students to not only read and understand the critical statements of the texts, but also to engage in a dialogue with those concepts. He asks the students to draw explicit connections between the text and the contemporary society in concrete ways. He speaks of a "laboratory of the imagination" (201), using science fiction (which, again, for him includes dystopian literature) as a means to begin a discussion that asks students to engage critically with the society that surrounds them. Calkins and McGhan speak of using a similar approach in the high school classroom.

> We believe that through experiences with the author's concept of the world explicated in his story, students can begin to develop and articulate notions of the world about them. The teen-age years seem to be the time in people's lives when they are most consciously concerned with who they are, what the world is like, and where they can and cannot go in it. By reading, discussing, and writing about the worlds projected in SF stories (which are often extrapolations of elements of today's world), they can grasp the idea that their world has elements which shape it, too. (84–85)

An essential element of Calkins and McGhan's pedagogy in the high school classroom is one that is mirrored across the other levels of instruction: they use these literatures to create an encounter wherein the student must begin to examine both self and his or her contemporary society. This is not to say that such pedagogy always goes smoothly, however. Kenneth Roemer recalls that one group of students he worked with were stymied by assignments in which they were asked to make those explicit connections. He says (echoing Anderson):

> This experience convinced me that many of my students were speculative illiterates. Their educational experiences had conditioned them primarily to be dependent on teachers-as-experts who gave them knowledge about the past and present which was legitimized when they gave it back to the teachers in appropriate oral and written forms. This exchange does involve learning, even empowerment: the students gain knowledge, and the teacher expands his or her sense of power by creating a mirror-like feedback situation. But such teaching does little to develop independent decision-making skills or to foster speculative thought processes

that can add significantly to students' abilities to measure themselves and their environments against alternative possibilities. (394)

Roemer is clearly frustrated by his students' seeming lack of subjunctive skills. He feels that speculation is both necessary and must be fostered at early levels of education. Although he is perhaps irresponsible in assuming that his students' problems all come from previous instructors, he is still self-reflexive. He goes on to say:

> My students' question also exposed my pedagogical illiteracy. I thought I knew how to teach students certain types of concepts, skills, and knowledge, but how could I answer their speculative illiteracy? How could I convince them of the value of what they brought to class (a necessary prerequisite for independent speculation), while simultaneously encouraging them to evaluate critically their ideals and values? How could I foster critical and speculative thought that would not be overly dependent upon the students' perceptions of my own values and ideals. I simply didn't know how to achieve these types of student "empowerment."
> And I'm still baffled. (394)

I think all instructors find themselves at a point like this. With the critical nature of student responses to science fiction and dystopian texts, such concerns do flare up. A solution, though, might be to remove the responsibility from the single student and move it to the group level. Though Robert Plank is an instructor who uses science fiction as a way to foster discussion and create context for psychology courses, he suggests another approach: group work. In his courses, he assigns texts, and then breaks students into small group discussions. Each group then has their reporter create a "speech" on their findings, which is passed to the instructor who then compiles the speeches and distributes them to the class later (162–64). The whole class then discusses what is on the compilation sheet. In this way, rather than each student being responsible for his or her own speculation, the group becomes the source of discussion, which can lead to further speculation. While Hall and Slade are right to point out that what adolescent readers actually *do* with the books we ask them to read can differ from what the aim (at least the marketing aims) of putting the book in front of them was to begin with, it is possible that they are getting *something* out of those readings (qtd. in Ames 15).

An Opening of Space

Before launching into that exploration, though, we should address the elephant in the room: there has been a long history of seeing texts intended for young people as only having value for their pedagogical potential. This cultural didactic imperative as it relates to YA books especially has been written about at length. As Basu, Broad, and Hintz state in their introduction to *Contemporary Dystopian Fiction for Young Adults*, "Writing for young people tends to balance the desire to please and instruct, *dulce et utile*, and this tension is particularly marked in YA dystopias. With their prescriptive qualities and unveiled moral messages, YA dystopian writing can seem preachy and even old fashioned" (5). They can seem quite preachy because, as Kay Sambell's assertion from 2003 states, "the 'adult' dystopia's didactic impact relies on the absolute, unswerving nature of its dire warning, the expression of moral meaning in the children's dystopia is often characterized by degrees of hesitation, oscillation, and ambiguity. In the adult dystopian vision, morally appealing heroes are unequivocally shown to fail" (164). She points this out in order to say that very often, in what she calls "the author's ethical duty to protect young readers' idealism," the writer of dystopian works for young readers is unwilling to extinguish hope entirely from the text (165).[9] Doing so undermines some of the impact of the dystopian warning, and this can lead to adverse critical reaction. Sambell goes on to say, though, that we might be witnessing a more "fluid style of didacticism in dystopian writing for children" (173). One that, she points out, allows for discussion and exploration, rather than simply hammers home an idea.

I don't want to fall back on that old cliché of seeing a text intended for young people as only its teachable message. And yet, how do we talk about YA dystopian texts *without* talking about their didactic characteristics, especially in a chapter where we are specifically talking about how these texts work within the classroom space? We might do so by following Sambell's thought, here, and suggesting ways that these texts open up discussion spaces rather than giving set-in-stone lesson plans.

Pressed into Service

We might also begin to think about the ways that these texts can be used in the classroom pedagogically. As I've been trying to assert, the use value of these texts lies in how instructors decide to use them in the classroom space.

Melissa Ames indicates in her 2013 article for *The High School Journal* that she believes YA dystopian literature might help students (especially American students) work through fears. She says,

> These narratives are important sites where the realities of a post-9/11 world are being worked out. Therefore, in consuming these texts, teenagers are likely working through fears lingering unconsciously perhaps years after the national trauma. Reading these books may not completely rewire the Millennial Generation, but it may find them contemplating some important societal problems including those that led up to the 9/11 terrorist attacks, as well as other less tragic concerns such as the effects of reality television, superficial beauty standards, and over-reliance on social technology. (Ames 17)

Perhaps, Ames suggests, we as educators might consider using dystopian literature in the classroom as a way to help students ease fears through discussion.[10]

David R. Dreyer suggests that we can use these texts to examine the field of international relations. "There is a growing body of literature on using fictional texts in the classroom to illustrate theories and concepts of international relations" (252). He believes that some students benefit more from using the fictionalized characters and nations of a text like *The Hunger Games* to examine what he calls the moral issues related to going to war and conducting war. Students connect to these characters more so than they might abstract concepts and "go beyond the surface and make connections between politics in Panem and politics in the real world" (264).

Jessica Seymour of Southern Cross University in Australia says that she feels we can use YA dystopias in the classroom to talk about a shift in masculinity. She reminds us that, "in literature, gender tends to be portrayed on a spectrum between very masculine and very feminine" (632).[11] She goes on to point out that the performance of masculinity is not limited to characters who identify as male. Further, she asserts that female characters are "often shown to perform hyper-masculinity, particularly in dystopian narratives where physical strength and pragmatism are portrayed as useful personality traits" (632). She notes that, ultimately, the ethic of care, that is to say an ethic of concern for the well-being of those around the character in question, which has come to be seen as a feminine set of ethics, is "ultimately portrayed as the most positive gender performance" (632).[12] So, while characters who identify as female are rupturing the gender binary by performing various forms of masculinities, Seymour sees that characters who identify as male are often rupturing that same binary by operating with an ethic of care. This has implications beyond just the upholding/rupturing of the stereotypical gender binary. Kimberly Reynolds points out that, when childhood is defined as a period of "dependency, passivity, weakness," these are stereotypically traits of femininity, and that when adolescence is defined as a period of time associated with the move toward agency through defiance of authority, adolescence is a kind of masculinity (73). Though this is not part of Seymour's exploration, one implication is that characters are not simply moving through the gender binary but also through a binary continuum from childhood to adolescence. Seymour also points out that she feels critics are quick to praise these female characters who embrace more traditionally masculine actions, but that there is little mention of the male characters' similarly boundary-pushing portrayals. While reading her article, I was reminded of the gender portrayals of the Gladers in *The Maze Runner*. The all-male society in the first three-fourths of that novel could have been depicted as a rehash of *Lord of the Flies*, with toxic masculinity run amuck, yet the society the boys have made is one of care. Consider the power of using these texts in classrooms with adolescents as a way of challenging societal gender binaries.

This follows along similar lines to Sarah Darer Littman's meditation on the ethics we encounter in the novel *Mockingjay*. Littman's essay draws parallels between her own experiences as a journalist during the invasion of Iraq by George Bush Jr. during the early 2000s and the experiences of Katniss during the later two books of the Hunger Games trilogy. During this time, she points out, many of her interactions with people seemed quite polarized. Some, she said, were of the belief that the ends justified the means when it came to gaining information regarding possible terrorist attacks or treatment of prisoners while others were shocked and horrified by the behavior that was being carried out in the name of their own country. In her essay, she shows that Katniss is constantly pulled between the poles of peace and war by her attachments to Peeta and Gale. Their attitudes push and pull on her own reasoning throughout the series. "Gale wants revenge at any cost, by any means necessary," she reminds us, but "Peeta is the one who, despite everything he's been through [. . .] is able to retain his essential humanity" (172). Do the ends justify the means in war, Littman asks us, or is it in that moment when we most want vengeance that we can show the most humanity? "That is why he's [meaning Peeta] the one that Katniss must end up with in order to stay true to herself and be able to heal and find some measure of happiness—happiness that Gale, with his moral ambivalence and quest for vengeance, could never have provided" (Littman 172).[13] At the core of the trilogy, when taken as a whole, is the question of how one behaves in the face of atrocity. Are revenge and justice the same thing, Collins's series asks us, according to Littman. Littman ends her essay by reminding us that, during an interview posted on the Scholastic website, when asked, Suzanne Collins said "she hoped that readers would come away with 'questions about how elements of the book might be relevant in their own lives. And, if they're disturbing, what they might do about them'" (Littman 177). Instructors could use Katniss's moral dilemma to ask students to consider what their own feelings are regarding revenge and forgiveness.[14]

Consider for a moment Amy Elliot's idea that Dashner's *The Maze Runner* is not only a dystopian work, but one that explores the ways trauma affects its characters. She says,

> Finding themselves at the intersection of trauma literature and dystopian literature, Dashner's audience can see the author both representing trauma and teaching his readers how to handle it, arming them with strategies to mitigate trauma's effects so that the dystopian future does not become a harsh reality. (180)

She goes further to say that she believes Dashner's work is a "proactive step" for readers by giving them tools to help them handle a future that is certain to have trauma in store (181). The Glader community, Elliot points out, is a community that is built on shared trauma. Showing a community that not only shares its trauma, but grows stronger through the sharing could allow readers (such as students in a classroom setting, or perhaps even patients in a group setting) to begin the process of dealing with their own trauma.

Elliot suggests, "Children growing up in the wake of trauma must navigate adult problems as they encounter their futures. Looking forward, perhaps young adults reading trauma literature will see both the destructive nature of trauma and the healing power" (196). Instructors could capitalize on this aspect of the text to begin discussions about trauma and how it affects society in the short and long term.

Jonathan Alexander and Rebecca Black suggest that one of the reasons certain young adult literature becomes more popular is because of the very educational environment that students live within in late-twentieth- and early twenty-first-century Western schools. In "The Darker Side of the Sorting Hat," Alexander and Black point out that, while students are being inundated with standardized tests, they find point of identification with dystopian worlds where there seem to be lots of tests occurring. In speaking of the series *The Hunger Games, Divergent, Legend,* and *The Testing,* they say,

> In this article, we examine how, in popular YA dystopian fiction, the types of selves promoted by testing, and their concomitant skills and abilities, largely serve the interests of the state by generating a passive and productive workforce to maintain the status quo. Resistance to that status quo is crucial to the plot of each series, but the imagination of such resistance in the novels emphasizes not just the difficulty but the personal *devastation* of working against dominant systems. (212)

This sense of the push and pull of institutionalized power on the identity of the adolescent represented in both the physical standardized test and the ideological goal of standardized testing is represented in many YA dystopian texts. It is not necessary for a text to have a science fiction setting for this tension to be represented, but within dystopian YA texts these tests are present.[15] Alexander and Black also point out that, "in spite of the extremely high social stakes associated with these tests [...] they are not designed to identify students' passions and interests. Instead the aptitude tests are geared toward identifying how these young people can be sorted into a group where they will be of the most use to society" (219). This creates a system in such texts where the representatives of the institutions of these societies, almost always adults, "only view and understand these children in highly instrumentalized ways. In essence, these young people exist only in the service of maintaining larger institutional structures, and the tests are designed to produce particular types of citizens to meet the needs of the state" (Alexander and Black 229). A person sorted into such a category via a test becomes identified with their results rather than what they see as their individual identity. A character might become "such a Hufflepuff" or "a typical Abnegation," and so on. It is through such an act of reduction that the institutions within that text begin to understand the character in question, and this must feel very familiar to students in the contemporary educational world. "For example, one crucial reaction to the economic downturn is a collateral shift in how young people understand their (increasingly limited) options for career and livelihood. Instead of cultivating personal pursuits, students likely feel the need to pursue more 'sure bets' or careers with more forecast economic stability" (Alexander and Black 229). Such moves are greeted with knowing nods from family and administrators, and they congratulate the young person for their "sound thinking." It is in this way, as Alexander and Black point out, that a YA text could come into the classroom as ways to help students begin to be more critical of even the educational institution itself or as prompts for discussion of issues such as contemporary economic pressures and how they affect education.

As Wang Xiaolan posits, "The issues explored by contemporary adolescent dystopian fiction can be roughly classified into three categories: response to the ethics concerning science and its application, anxiety over contemporary environmental catastrophes, and reflection of war and its destructive effect" (79).[16] I agree with Xiaolan when she points out that the first category "is a common motif in the totalitarian dystopian fiction [...] the rulers suppress individual will or personal wish in the name of public welfare" (79). The ethical dilemma of how technology/science is used in relation to the political power of the regime is one of the primary discussions these texts intend to have. "The scientific and technological achievement is meant to bring about convenience and comfort to the people, but it eventually provides the rulers with convenient tools for mental surveillance and psychic control" (Xiaolan 80). This is, after all, the very thing that Cory Doctorow's novels, such as *Little Brother*, with its discussion of RFID tags and content laws, attempt to do. Again, while Kimberley Reynolds's work is not a part of Xiaolan's inquiry, we might use her assertion to further flesh out such an exploration by students. Reynolds says that she believes technology in children's literature typically shows up in one of three ways: (1) what she calls "Prometheus" stories, where humanity's search for tech goes beyond some ethical line of what "ought" to be known and the result is destruction, (2) what Reynolds calls "Frankenstein" stories, where humans have "played god" and AI or androids were created and something goes wrong, or (3) stories of technological reliance that causes a degradation in human quality of life which Reynolds calls "technological dystopias" (164). Through these texts, students could be asked to think of the ways that their technology might be used against them, or ways that their reliance on technology might cause harm to culture over all.[17] Xiaolan goes so far as to use the metaphor of an inoculation, suggesting that the YA dystopian text is "the kind of atmosphere with floating virus or bacteria, which helps them to improve their mental immunity and prepare them well for the future life in adulthood" (86). Using Reynolds's and Xiaolan's ideas alongside well-selected texts in the classroom might create an atmosphere where students begin to critique their own technological reliance issues as well as come up with strategies for critical intervention.

Consider for a moment that we might even use these texts as a way to ask students to examine the very spaces where these discussions are happening. The architecture of the contemporary American high school is often described as "institutional" but in many ways it could also be described as dystopian. Kerry Freedman asks us to consider that

> there is another type of architecture that diminishes people and resists human engagement in an industrial environment intended for social control. This type is easily seen in large-scale work environments or institutional architecture, such as schools. Most public high school architecture has characteristics similar to prison architecture, such as a lack of windows, cement walls, long hallways that direct people into small rooms, and few public gathering spaces or lounge areas. The environment created through the design of many such schools emphasize social control, but it is often the neglect of this architecture, particularly in urban and lower socioeconomic areas, that can be most oppressive. And, when schools and their local communities are in this condition, students cannot walk away from this dystopian aesthetic. (8)

Though the thrust of Freedman's argument is about how neglect of the school buildings themselves creates a dystopian and oppressive aesthetic, the Foucauldian institutional nature of the learning environment is also part of the discussion. Freedman points out that students can begin to use the awareness gained from dystopian works and discussions to begin to raise their voices and critique the spaces that they are forced to exist in on a daily basis.

There is still a great deal of resistance to seeing young adult literature as anything more than empty entertainment from administrators and parents alike. This resistance is doubled when the texts come from genre fiction, which is still seen by so many as the most empty of hollow entertainment, despite the highly critical natures of the works.

Expanding the Universe

I belong in the camp that uses science fiction and dystopian literatures for their critical natures. More specifically, I find myself very much in agreement with Calkins and McGhan: young adult science fiction and dystopian literature for young people can help adolescents who are already doing the extremely important work of identity formation. The genres can be especially helpful in this by allowing critical discussion and fostering awareness within the classroom setting.[18] Instructors can set up assignments that allow students to speculate, either in discussion or by creating original works of SF or dystopian lit, in order for this work to occur. For example, an instructor might consider creating collaborative assignments, as well, in order to make sure that speculation occurs rather than being stymied by fear of the power structure within the classroom. An instructor who uses these genres in the classroom must be aware that with the fostering of critical awareness that can (and hopefully will) occur when students encounter these texts, some anger, confusion, and possibly even backlash might occur. An important aspect of any pedagogy using science fiction or dystopian literature, then, must be to deconstruct the power relationships within the classroom space as often as possible. As Samuelson writes, his students found it most helpful when he was one more member of the discussion rather than the top of the power pyramid.

Since both science fiction and dystopian literature are inherently critical genres, the student who studies them must be allowed a space to be critical of prevailing thought. As instructors, teachers, and librarians, I believe that we should allow these readers such a space rather than being overly concerned with the goal of upholding the status quo over emerging critical concerns. As educators using these tools in our classrooms, encouraging critical inquiry and exploration is an important goal. Instructors, then, should be concerned with recognizing the difference between genuinely critical exploration and what we might call rebellion for rebellion's sake. I do not mean to devalue the letting-off-of-steam that can occur when a student at any level finally gets or creates the chance to speak back to power; far from it—I consider that a valuable action, particularly during adolescence. However, it is important not to mistake what my mother would likely refer to as "sass" for sustained, critical examination and response. After all, good teaching, bell hooks tells us, should "enable transgressions" (12). It should be an "insurgent intellectual practice" (11). I wish to propose here that the goal of teaching should be to enable students to make those transgressions—to provide them with the critical tools that they need to carry out their own insurgency. The goal should be to help them make visible the often invisible formative ideologies circulating in our culture. Once the course is through, then, students will ideally be left in a better position to decide what they believe or don't believe.

Bracher identifies critical pedagogy as teaching theory that "aims at liberation from the oppressive forces and structures that constitute racism, classism, colonialism, and sexism. But in addition to liberating students (and others), it also aims to help them develop their full potentials, become empowered" (110). This is very much in keeping with Paolo Freire's understanding that the path to that power for both student and instructor is to resist the traditions that have caused oppression within the classroom. Our goal should be, as Freire points out, the restoration of the "humanity of both" (26). Engaged instructors enter into the act of teaching open to the possibility of learning just as much as they teach. Likewise, the student, as Bracher points out, has needs to be met that can be at odds with the needs of the instructor. Learning should be the dance of negotiation between these needs and not merely a one-way power gradient. Freire reminds us of this in his rejection of the now-famous banking model (53): he enjoins against treating students as merely empty vessels to be filled with information, a process that dehumanizes both them *and* the instructor. Here is where we as instructors run up against difficulty: how can instructors design content that engages students with the material and shows them the use and value of the tools we are offering, without conceiving of the students as empty receptacles? Freire says that truly liberating education consists of "acts of cognition, not transferals of information" (60). He suggests that we conceive of the act of educating as problem-posing (65), a praxis of pointing out the gaps in things and engaging in thought experiment. "To achieve this goal," he goes further, "the oppressed must confront reality critically, simultaneously objectifying and acting upon that reality. A mere perception of reality not followed by this critical intervention will not lead to a transformation of objective reality" (34). While I have some trouble with his conceptualizing of a singular, objective reality, I agree that our goal should be in helping students, as they help us in return, to a critical understanding of our own assumptions of reality. This will ultimately facilitate the re-humanization of both parties in the awakening from the concept of unconstructed reality to a notion of the constructed-ness of self and reality, codetermined. This is the praxis of teaching.

Practical Explorations

In 2008, I taught an undergraduate literature course in science fiction and dystopian literature with the goal of not only fostering an appreciation of the two genres, but also teaching students to *see* the differences clearly. In keeping with this, my course focused on reading dystopian literature and science fiction side by side in order to show that, although they are often considered the same thing, both are unique genres doing particular socio-critical work. I wanted to help students see that in some genres, authors function as social critics, and that through studying texts in these genres, students might be able to view their own subject formations via ideology.

Initially, the questions I wanted to research were these: how do undergraduate students view science fiction? How do undergraduate students view dystopian fiction? And how can dystopian fiction help undergraduate students view their own subject formation via ideology? What I wanted to observe were the particular issues that students encounter while examining differences between these two genres, something not emphasized in most classroom encounters. This course was designed to help students become more informed consumers of these genres and the particular work that each genre does. In keeping with that, I separated out the course into two sections taking roughly seven weeks each to cover (1) history and concepts of science fiction, and (2) history and concepts of dystopian literature.

The students studied the unique grammar of science fiction that creates the cognitive estrangement allowing the author to explore the encounter with the other. They then explored the ideological frameworks exposed by the dystopian work. The science fiction texts we read were *Have Spacesuit Will Travel* by Robert Heinlein, *Be More Chill* by Ned Vizzini, and a 2007 graphic novel adaptation of *20,000 Leagues Under the Sea* by Jules Verne. The dystopian works were *1984* by George Orwell, *The Giver* by Lois Lowry, and *Fahrenheit 451* by Ray Bradbury. In conjunction with those texts, we watched *Stargate* as part of the science fiction texts, as well as clips from *2001: A Space Odyssey*, *The Fifth Element*, *Alien*, *The Day the Earth Stood Still*, and *Forbidden Planet*. As part of the dystopian section of texts, we also watched George Lucas's film *THX 1138*, and Terry Gilliam's *Brazil*. Of those texts, Vizzini's *Be More Chill* and Lowry's *The Giver* are both intended for young adults; specifically, Vizzini's novel is YA SF, while Lowry's is a dystopian work.

I started off the dystopian literature section by asking them to think about utopia and dystopia as opposites. I also wanted them to begin the process of seeing that ideology is present in many places that they do not normally consider it to be. This included destabilizing the concept that "a law is absolute," which paid off later as we discussed the various rules, laws, and mores throughout the texts.

Language use is an important part of dystopian literature and the formative ideologies of the ISAs within those texts. I decided, as a way to get students thinking about how language adjusts perception and possibility of being, to get them to do a language activity. The activity consisted of a series of slips of paper given at approximately ten-minute intervals to each group. The first slip said: "1. In the space provided, pick any noun (a rose, a dog, a house, etc.) and describe it in 20 words that do not repeat the name of the noun." The second slip said: "2. Now, in the space below describe that same noun in 10 words that do not repeat the name of the noun." Slip three said: "3.

In the space below, describe that same noun in 5 words that do not repeat the name of the noun." And finally, the fourth slip said: "4. Finally, describe that same noun in 3 words that do not repeat the name of the noun."

This activity seemed to help them to "back into" Orwell's concept of Newspeak by showing them that once a group starts making decisions about a word's meaning, the more they cut away from the possibilities of that meaning, the fewer possibilities exist for creating new meaning. They were forced to decide on some criteria. I think they were surprised by the fact that they had made a decision like that without much discussion. Most groups also reported that the words that made the final list had been on their lists since the twenty word variations. What was also really interesting to me is that only one group used sentences instead of listing characteristics. However, by the second pass, even that group reverted to a list format rather than sentences.

Of course, Newspeak is not the only difficult concept for twenty-first-century Americans to grasp when it comes to Orwell's novel. The trouble most students had with Orwell's *1984* was the question of why Winston doesn't leave Oceania. After all, the life the Proles lead seems to agree with him—why not simply just leave the party to join them? I made reference to these "patrols" we were constantly told are at work in that area, but still—students find it difficult to believe that a character can't simply self-actualize by walking away from an adverse situation. I had to ask them more than once to set aside the ideals that come from being a twenty-first-century American and to remember that the society Winston was raised in is quite different, ideologically. I also reminded them that when someone is socialized to believe that they are always under the power of another group, there is no escape concept in their mind—nowhere to go. Even when Winston is defying the party, he fully assumes he will be caught. Why, if he could make it to the Prole town and even to places outside the city, could he not escape Oceania entirely? My students seemed to find this, of all the critical questions that arose from our reading, the most disturbing. Several students expressed outright disgust with Winston's inability to commit to escape. There may be many reasons for this reaction from them, but I believe that this caused a powerful moment of ideological recognition for my students. If he had the desire to escape, they asked, why did he not? It is precisely that problem that I raised in the course. We examined the bedrock foundational belief that the students as fairly typical American individuals in the twenty-first century seem to have: that freedom is worth sacrificing all for. One thing became immediately apparent—that they had never questioned whether or not this belief was a construct. My goal in asking them to examine this belief was not to demand that they adopt a counter-belief, however. I feel it is of utmost importance that students not be asked to examine their ideological constructions merely to have me demand they take on new constructions that are to my liking. Nonetheless, the very question unsettled them.

By comparison, students seemed much more comfortable examining Lois Lowry's *The Giver*. Perhaps because of Jonas's escape at the end, they were able to identify with him much easier than they identified with Winston from Orwell's novel. Many students grasped the underlying metaphor of Lowry's novel: utopia = childhood, escape from utopia = adolescence. Students, formed in contemporary American ideological concepts of freedom, were far more able to connect to Jonas than Winston Smith from *1984* because of Jonas's escape. Other students were more interested in the ideological elements of control (ISAs) that were shown within the novel. In order to maintain the infantilized population that makes the "utopia" exist, strong emotions are not only devalued ideologically, but suppressed through medication.[19] Utopia = childhood is an equation that works only in the sense of the romantic conception of childhood being an idealized time of sweetness and gentleness. Another element of control that students picked up on within the text was the ideology of immovable jobs or social status within society.

I also asked them to imagine themselves a teacher in the world of the novel *1984*. I asked them to consider the pedagogical implications of the "2 minutes of hate." You may recall this is the mandatory gathering of all citizens around a large telescreen where images of the main enemy of the state, almost always Emmanuel Goldstein, are projected and the audience is encouraged (or, from Smith's perspective, forced) to demonstrate their hatred to extremes. I asked them to consider what their students might be getting from a lesson such as this. With some prodding, we eventually got to the idea that those participating in the moment were creating a firm boundary between themselves and the object of the hatred, and that these imaginary students would be shoring up their identities as "good citizens" by making sure that there was always a "bad citizen" to hate. The students and I then discussed, as we have earlier, how this is a way to create the docile citizen the fictional repressive regime wishes to see—give the masses someone to other. I then asked them to consider a text more rooted in science fiction as a mode, such as *Stranger in a Strange Land* by Heinlein. We discussed how Valentine Smith is an O/other but because he is our protagonist, we come to know him. The boundaries that are erected because of his fantastical powers are broken down because we can read his thoughts, understand his intentions even when they seem on the outside to be hostile. My intention was to show the students, as I have maintained, that the goal of these two genres are at somewhat cross purposes: one aims to show how power is maintained through othering, while the other aims to show the encounter with the other.

In the end, I believe that the students came to understand the differences between the two genres, but the journey was far from an easy one. My hope is that they not only came to understand these genres as separate, but that on some level the texts brought them to an understanding of the political. It is a popular stereotype to say that "millennials" are a disengaged generation, that they are completely uninterested in the political process. To return to Melissa

Ames's thoughts, though, adolescents' intense interest in dystopian literature may point in the exact opposite direction. Ames says,

> the reading preferences of this generation indicate that this label of "apolitical" may not be as fitting as some believe. In fact, the popularity of young adult dystopia, which is ripe with these political themes, suggests that this group is actually quite interested in these topics, although they often turn to the safe confines of fiction to wrestle with them. (3)

Ames points out that there are a number of scholars who have suggested the use of dystopian literature in the classroom. As Ames reminds us,

> Glasglow (2001) encouraged utilizing dystopian novels in social justice units. She argued that "social justice education has the potential to prepare citizens who are sophisticated in their understanding of diversity and group interaction, able to critically evaluate social institutions, and committed to working democratically with diverse others" (p. 54). (17)

As we have discussed here, by examining the problems of the fictional society, parallels can be drawn to the real society that exists outside the text (and, indeed, beyond the classroom door). Ames also reminds us that Wolk "stated that reading dystopian novels allows 'students to question the world we have and envision a better world we could have' because these texts 'offer unique opportunities to teach these habits of mind.'" The questioning is an important part of the pedagogical process for use with these texts. The genre is uniquely suited to engaging these questions for the reader. Ames then quotes Collins, Groenke, Rose-Shafer, and Zenzano's 2006 article, "Teacher to Teacher: What Texts Effectively Raise Issues Related to 9/11 for Secondary Students?," in which they point out that teachers are in a unique position to "select texts that will help students to critically examine the world and media representations of it [. . .] However, these texts can do more than just prompt students to examine the world—they can be used as the catalyst to incite real action" (17). With a shift from "how would someone within this society change what was happening?" to the question, "how would you change something going on in our society that bothers you?" those conversations can begin.

Ames finishes her thought by pointing out,

> This literary trend indicates that while these young readers may be disheartened by contemporary politics and under-informed in current events, they are not uninterested in the social problems that underlie both. The success of these novels implies that teenagers are willing to entertain societal critiques—even ones that implicate themselves. Rather than being a problematic discrepancy, the "mismatch" between the reading interests of young adults and their direct political action suggests that young adults could easily be molded into more politically engaged citizens. (17)

As she suggests, perhaps creating situations in which their concerns are more regularly addressed, such as the classroom space, especially when using dystopian works as a proxy to help begin their exploration of how to discuss these political issues, could allow for a shift for the adolescent from disheartened and silenced to engaged and active. We can use the classroom as a somewhat-safer space to begin that process of engagement with social issues to give the students tools they need to enter the larger, and often much more contentious (as well as dangerous) conversation at large.

5

"Signs of Life": Considerations for the Future of the Genres and Their Critique

In the audio commentary track to the 2017 film, *The Space Between Us*, director Peter Chelsom recounts that during pre-production and filming, cast and crew would sometimes refer to the film as "the fault in our Mars." This is, of course, a reference to the 2014 film adaptation of the 2012 John Green YA novel titled *The Fault in Our Stars*. The reference is an acknowledgment that *The Space Between Us* not only has adolescent protagonists going through the pains of *bildungsroman*, but that this drama, whether it is set in space or on Earth, shares many similarities.[1] Twenty seventeen is the year that *Star Trek* returned after more than a decade away from the small screen, and that Seth MacFarlane, creator of *Family Guy*, decided it was the right time to realize one of his lifelong dreams, which was to bring a *Star Trek*-style science fiction show to TV.[2] This was also the time that Ridley Scott returned to science fiction, creating prequels to one of his masterworks, *Alien*, and a sequel to his other masterwork, *Blade Runner*.[3] At the same time, the popular Internet site YouTube chose the 2016 film *The Thinning* for its new Red subscription service. This film revisits the idea of testing young people and purging (at least seemingly) those who do not achieve highly enough on the tests from the society—a major trope of the YA dystopia genre. All of this occurring, of course, in a resurgence of interest in Margaret Atwood's 1985 dystopian novel, *The Handmaid's Tale*, which now features prominently as a live-action television show on the streaming service, Hulu.

At the same time as these new films, shows, and books are being produced, we must acknowledge that the massive trend that the dystopian genre enjoyed has slowed to a trickle compared to what it once was. And we are still left with what we might call a glut of texts from the period of time when the trend occurred, as well.[4] While many dystopian and science fiction texts, such as *Hunger Games* and *I Am Number 4*, received quite a lot of attention and even became films, there are others that are also important that received little to no critical attention at all, such as *Unwind* and *The Unnaturalists*. We need to take the time to examine these texts thoroughly from a critical point of view in what we might perhaps call hindsight now that we have some time to consider them. I believe that our exploration of these texts is truly just beginning. Not only is there still interest in using these genres to explore the human condition, but also specific interest in using these genres to explore the experiences for young people, and I believe that even with the fantastic work that has already been done on these texts, we have only just begun to explore the importance and meaning of the mass of texts that were produced during that trend.

What directions might we take moving forward, then? As I've said, I think we might reexamine some of the work we've already done based on a closer look at the concept of dystopian literature, and also by diving more deeply into the ways that the examination of YA science fiction and YA dystopian literature combine with contemporary fields of study. What happens when we examine the role of diversity in the YA SF and YA dystopian genres even more closely than we already have? Further, what happens when we begin to divide YA dystopian work from other similar but not the same genres?

The Unidentified

In her brilliant essay, "The Future Is Pale: Race in Contemporary Young Adult Dystopian Novels," Mary J. Couzelis writes,

> Carrie Hintz and Elaine Ostry believe that "utopian literature encourages young people to view their society with a critical eye, sensitizing or predisposing them to political action." However this is not always the case. Not all utopian and dystopian fiction creates worlds where readers reflect on their contemporary society, and especially not to the point of considering action. (133)

While it might seem that she is refuting the idea that I hold central here, that is, that for a text to be classified as dystopian it *must* cause the reader to reflect upon the society in which they live, her main point is that even in the most thoughtful of dystopian writing, some of the ideologies that underpin a fictional society might not be as thoroughly critiqued as others. Her point is specifically that, while encouraging young people to focus critical eyes on governmental policies within the text and, by extension, in their own world, some dystopian works ignore other issues, such as race (and, I would include, sexual identity politics), causing those ideologies to be re-inscribed on the reader. Her point, specifically, is about the lack of characters who are anything but white in so many of the YA dystopian texts we see on the market. "By maintaining narrative silence about this contemporary issue, these novels perpetuate the hegemonic status quo of pretending race does not matter, which only privileges the dominant race" (Couzelis 132).

In this book, I have not included much theoretical work that has been done on race or theories on sexual identity. I recognize that leaves me open to critique on this front. However, my intention with this omission was two-fold: One, to provide a kind of bedrock theory onto which other theories might then be used to extend one's examination. For instance, how are the RSAs used to enforce racial policies within the world of a dystopian work? Or how might one use Adilufu Nama's poignant racial theory regarding the coding of the other as hegemonic white culture's fear of blackness to then examine the lack of diversity of race in YA SF—can we see this as a fulfillment of a desire to eradicate black youth on the part of white culture and its view of the future? Two, to point toward other critics who are doing that work with hopes that the reader will seek them out directly, giving them voice rather than co-opting that voice. Seek out such voices as Suzanne Roszak's brilliant article on hybridity, "Coming of Age in a Divided City: Cultural Hybridity and Ethnic Injustice in Sandra Cisneros and Veronica Roth"[5] or Lynette James's fantastic article about native identities in science fiction and dystopian literature, "Children of Change, Not Doom: Indigenous Futurist Heroines in YA"[6] or Adilufu Nama's brilliant book, *Black Space*. In other words, I see the tools that I propose here not as an attempt to ignore the importance of radical examination of ideologies of identity and/or race, but as tools that might help a reader who is using those other theorists rather than as tools that supplant those voices. I leave that space blank not as a way to elide responsibility, but as a way of leaving that space open for those tools to be used alongside these.

By way of suggesting how that might work, I ask you to consider the stereotypical American high school experience of the late twentieth century.[7] The newfound rigidity of rules combined with a more open schedule. The simultaneous rigidity and openness of the social structure as the student experiments with different identities and the peer groups that come with those identities. The emphasis is on standardized testing and how that impacts the adolescents' sense of self as well as the reactions it produces in the adults and the system around them. When viewed at just the right angle (which may very well be the angle directors call a "Dutch tilt"), this starts to look like a dystopian novel, though it is what we call real life.

I bring this up because what we may be seeing in YA dystopian novels as I've defined them here, is not teens reacting with horror to some bleak future, but instead the young adult reader finding something all too familiar to relate to. Consider for a moment that, in some ways, from the right angle, isn't a teen character's ordeal in a Hunger Game just a reflection of what the young adult reader experiences in the lunch room? Speaking on the subject of why teens, and especially teen girls, are attracted to dystopian texts that adults have complained are "too violent" in 2014, Jan Susina said, "While adults may find these books shocking and overtly violent, young adults are less troubled by those elements and see these texts as reflections of their world. I think these books reveal that many young adults have a rather bleak outlook toward the future" (qtd. in Hatch).

Remember that the world they live in is already a dystopian one in which their rights are trampled daily through macro- or micro-aggressions. This is especially true if the adolescent happens to be LGBT+. Consider for a moment that so-called conversion therapy is still legal in many states. A teen could find themselves very quickly shipped off (sometimes to places outside the boundaries of the continental United States) where their rights are stripped from them and only returned should they undergo some change in their core sexual identity. This is not the plot of some dystopian novel, this is present day. This is happening to a teen right now, somewhere, as your read this sentence.

The Apocalyptic Dividing Line

Not only is there confusion as to whether or not dystopian texts should be seen as a category of text in their own right or as a sub-genre or science fiction, as we've discussed, but there also seems to be an issue with what exactly comprises a dystopian text.[8] I recognize that, as others point out, the roots of the word dystopia come to mean "a place where one wouldn't want to be." However, as I have pointed out, there is a long tradition of dystopian texts in print, and the texts that seem to fit most easily into this category tend to share one thing in common: a sense of totalitarian fascism. While there is a lot of what we might think of as wiggle room in that definition, there is something of a boundary there we can see.

Some of the confusion likely comes from the fact that many dystopias, in order to wipe away our current society that, it is assumed, would never allow itself to be overrun by fascists who wish to monitor and control every aspect of our lives, create some apocalypse that then necessitates a remaking of society. It is within that remaking of society postapocalypse that the element of surveillance and control creep in. The fictional dictators often accomplish this with the rhetoric of "for your own safety" immediately followed by "in order to prevent something like this happening again." It is then that the fictional society puts in place both physical and rhetorical tools, both functioning together like nets to "catch" its members and turn them back toward the society, for control of its citizens. As a critic, one must ask themselves what role that fictional apocalypse plays in the overall narrative. In the case of dystopian works, it is often there only to clear the stage for the "new" society that has at its heart the surveillance state. If the apocalypse is the central focus, then the warning is often an environmental one, which would take the book in a different, more ecocritical, direction. We shouldn't say that simply because a book takes place postapocalypse that it is a dystopia.

Consider the case of the 2013 film, *After Earth*. One might be tempted, using some of the other definitions that have been suggested, upon seeing the film to classify it as dystopian since its central conceit is that the Earth, very far in the future, has become hostile to human life. It might further be tempting for some critics to classify it as YA dystopian because the central protagonist is a teenage boy. But I do think it might be in our interest to reexamine the film through a different lens in order to demonstrate once more the boundary between the two genres. I propose that we look at the film not as a big-budget science fiction film intended for a mostly adult audience (which was how it was marketed and, subsequently, why it failed so miserably at the box office), and instead look at the film through the lens of science fiction intended for an adolescent audience. That is to say, that perhaps, instead of showing something allegorically about the adult world to adults, the film has at its heart a more prescriptive and didactic intent. I believe that reconsidering the film in this way puts it in a better light.

The plot of the film is relatively straightforward. An unnamed environmental apocalypse happens during the twenty-first century and humans have to leave Earth. Nova Prime is the name given to the planet that humans settle on first. A thousand or so years later, a race called the S'Krell come to Nova Prime with intent to conquer. Their primary weapons are genetically modified creatures called Ursas who can sense fear. The humans are protected by a group called the Ranger Corps, led by Will Smith's character, General Cypher Raige. The general leads the humans to victory, defeating the invasion, but during the fighting, Raige's young son, Kitai (Jaden Smith's character), and his daughter, Senshi, are attacked. Senshi dies while Kitai looks on. The boy grows up blaming himself for not being able to defend his sister. Kitai applies to join the rangers to make himself stronger and, in some sense, to make up to his father for what he feels was his inability to defend his sister. The problem is that Kitai, though he wants to be, simply isn't that good a ranger. He tends to be reckless and not follow commands, and so the general sees his son as something of a failure and a disappointment. The general embarks on one last tour before retirement and his wife, Faia, convinces him to take Kitai with him as a last-ditch effort she hopes will bond them. During the trip, an uncharted asteroid field damages the ship and the only place to set down is on Earth, which is now off-limits, a quarantined world. The ship crash-lands killing all but the general and Kitai. The general is severely wounded and cannot move, and the ship's emergency beacon is in a portion of the ship which has crashed quite a distance from the section the general and Kitai are in. Because of this, the general has to help Kitai to go out into the long-abandoned ecosystem of Earth so that he can traverse the distance and activate the emergency beacon. During his journey to do so, the general is constantly feeding information and instructions to Kitai's earpiece, but the decisions on what to do to handle the various animals and plants that he encounters, many of them extremely hostile, are up to Kitai. Eventually the boy and his father reach a crisis point where they must negotiate the boy's level of autonomy and the film ends with the boy successfully making it to the tail section of the spaceship, defeating the Ursa that was secretly being transported onboard the ship and got loose during the crash, and activating the emergency beacon. The boy is now bonded with his father, though somewhat shakily. If you're thinking, "that all sounds a little familiar," you wouldn't be wrong.

The Ursa creatures, a human word that means, of course, "bear," form an integral part of the metaphor. They are perfect weapons for the invading race because they have been evolved to sense the hormones given off by humans who are experiencing the fight-or-flight response. They "smell" fear. The general, again, Will Smith's character, was able to defeat them because he found a way to "ghost," which is to say, to control his fear to a level where the fight-or-flight response doesn't occur. Kitai struggles with that skill—struggles to control his fear. The key to the metaphor at the heart of the story, then, is a boy who has lead a somewhat sheltered life suddenly having to go into a harsh alien environment and survive. He has his father for advice, via an armband communication device, but Kitai himself must make decisions that affect his safety minute by minute. They spend a great deal of the film struggling about Kitai's level of autonomy.

The plot of the film dresses up some very familiar tropes in science fiction costumes. *After Earth* exists within a tradition of stories intended for adolescents that involve sending the adolescent (usually male) character out into the wilderness as a means of teaching them something. The narrator or focal character moves from the comfortable world of civilization into the wilderness and there learns something about existence which we assume they would not have learned in the more structured world they came from. When they return to that world, then (as most, but not all, do), we perceive in them a growth. We could spend hours tracing the literary genealogy of this theme/plot, but for our purposes let's start with 1959's *My Side of the Mountain* by Jean Craighead George. Remember that this book is the story of Sam Gribley, who runs off to the Catskills to attempt to live by himself for a year. At one point, seeing his father approaching after so long a time apart, Sam thinks, "For a long moment, I stood wondering whether to meet Dad or run forever. I was self-sufficient. I could travel the world over, never needing a penny, never asking anything of anyone" (George 173).

Gary Paulsen's 1987 book, *Hatchet*, serves as another signpost on this particular road. *Hatchet*, you'll recall, is the story of thirteen-year-old Brian Robeson, who is on his way to visit his father when the plane carrying him crashes. He spends fifty-four days attempting to survive in the harsh Canadian wilderness using only the titular hatchet, a gift from his mother, to survive. Upon his rescue, he emerges from the forest with a newfound sense of empowered self-sufficiency and maturity.

Of course, we must include 2001's *Touching Spirit Bear* by Ben Mikaelsen. In this book, Cole Matthews is sent into the wilderness as a punishment/form of therapy. He is banished to a remote island off the coast of Alaska. There, he comes across an enormous white bear, which he battles. He emerges from the battle and the experience with a newfound maturity and empathy.

I recognize I am pushing somewhat to define these books as YA. Most would be more comfortable calling them middle school readers. However, consider that each involves a young boy moving from their somewhat comfortable place to the wilderness and then coming back into society with a newfound sense of identity. Is this not the definition we use for at least one of the ways we think about the adolescent's struggle?

To pick up another thread, *After Earth* is also a postapocalyptic narrative. We can put it in the category of the proliferation of postapocalyptic narratives from the late 2000s/early 2010s. During the first ten years of the two thousands, American culture became obsessed with postapocalyptic narratives, mainly in the form of zombie fiction (though, the ecological disaster narrative also loomed large in our imaginations). Hintz and Ostry, Bradford and colleagues, and Fredric Jameson are all in agreement as to why this might be; though some large-scale disaster is often necessary to wipe away the "old" society (us) in order to make room for the "new" society of the narrative in both utopian and dystopian writing, there is a category of post-disaster narrative which either has not or will never lead to utopia/dystopia. Fredric Jameson comments that "we probably need another term to characterize the increasingly popular visons of total destruction and of the extinction of life on Earth which seem more plausible than the Utopian vision ... but also rather different from the various catastrophes (including the old ban-the-bomb anxieties of the 1950s) prefigured in critical dystopias." Bradford and colleagues point out that a large portion of these post-catastrophe texts tend to be ecological in their scope, saying, "The Devastation caused by pollution and habitat destruction have become a primary catalyst for new world (dis-)order in the post-disaster narratives which have taken the place of the nuclear holocausts of Cold War–era fiction, and in such narratives ecopoiesis is grounded in dystopian settings and themes" (90).

We could say that there exists a kind of ecocritical postapocalyptic science fiction, but there might also be a segment of that sub-subgenre that uses the devastated ecology as metaphor to stage other metaphors. We might consider some of Slavoj Žižek's thoughts on the apocalypse and its relation to the end-cycle of late capitalism.

When thinking about the proliferation of disaster narratives, Žižek mirrors Kübler-Ross in many ways by suggesting five stages in which one might deal with what he calls the "forthcoming apocalypse," with the fifth stage being "after passing through this zero point, the subject no longer perceives the situation as a threat, but as the chance of a new beginning" (xi–xii), or acceptance. I suggest perhaps we as audience are also involved in this way of thinking.

The allegory of the disaster narrative, especially the ecological postapocalyptic narrative, is one of loss and mourning in some cases, but also of a chance at a new beginning.

In the case of *After Earth*, we see this played out as an accidental return to the very planet where those systems were birthed and then wiped away. Kitai's return to Earth is the moving forward from the zero point of the apocalypse, which happened conveniently off stage. We are spared the horror of watching Earth die away, and also the boredom of watching it regrow. Instead, we are left with the wonder (is this not the same principle on which Cameron's *Avatar* functioned?) of a seemingly newfound world which is, in fact, our own. One can go home again, once that home has been destroyed and rebuilt, that is.

So, we can see that the apocalypse in any given narrative may be a way for the author to clear the decks, create a new space for the allegory to play out. In this case, then, what might the hostile posthuman world Earth has become be an allegory for in "After Earth?" To understand that, I believe we must pull together one more thread before finally coming to understand.

As we discussed, science fiction is the ideal place to explore othered subjectivity. I believe that the genre of science fiction is a perfect medium for this message. One of the primary characteristics of science fiction, Darko Suvin tells us, is the use of cognitive estrangement to defamiliarize some element of our own culture in order to see it more clearly. So, in almost all science fiction, we can speak of the coding. What element of our world is being metaphorized via the narrative so that we may see it more clearly by, somewhat counterintuitively, divorcing it from many of its contexts. Instead of a narrative where a contemporary parent and child are arguing about the use of the car on the weekend, we get Graff and Ender Wiggen arguing about autonomy within the context of the Battle School zero-G games. It is in this way that the familiar is defamiliarized enough, is cognitively estranged enough, for us to see it anew. Sands and Frank theorize that this is one of the essential differences between science fiction intended for children and that intended for young adults. They say, "Whereas children's science fiction series attempt in various ways to make the unknowable known, young adult science fiction series—despite retaining familiarity through constant characters—make the familiar into something strange and unknown" (28). I would press that further by saying that this binary relationship of estrangement to text is not merely a condition of serialized fiction for young audiences, but is in fact a generalized genre characteristic. Sands and Frank say, the idea is to make the child comfortable with the unknown. We see this manifested in such things as a family trip into space for a picnic on the moon, or a robot who acts like a little boy. For young adults, however, the object is to make the reader unfamiliar enough with things that are commonplace as a way to see them anew. We see this manifested in such tropes as the teacher who turns out to be an alien. "[T]hus, series science fiction for children, despite its often alien settings or characters, contains a considerable amount of recognizable and/or comforting material for the young audience" (Sands and Frank 23), and in science fiction intended for young adults we see much less material designed to comfort the reader. The choices they make in the forest and how they come out of it represent the distancing of the familiar, thus this is YA.

The Earth Kitai has returned to is a representation of the mythopoetic undisturbed wilderness as the film traffics in the same untouched wilderness = opportunity for growth allegory as the young adult books I mentioned. A human being faces the homeworld as a complete stranger to what it has become. This creates that moment of cognitive dissonance for us as an audience—Kitai's alien-ness, though he looks like a human being, allows us to see the world through his distanced eyes. Further, this may all function as a metaphor for the change in sociopolitical climate that we face in the early twenty-first century—a change so profound that even the most experienced parent (represented by General Cypher Raige) can only sit by and watch while their child goes out into unknown dangers, facing them on their own. Cypher's continued admonition to his son to root himself in the present moment is the only piece of information/wisdom that ends up being useful despite there being a lot the general says to his son. We understand that we cannot guarantee them a future. Kitai must make his way in this new world with a familiar name by himself. The information and wisdom from the past can only be a loose and distant guide, not a set of rules. All of this, then, is intended to represent the growth of the character from relatively pampered child to capable adolescent.

"After Earth," then, is YA postapocalyptic ecocritical science fiction that does NOT fit into the dystopian trend which these narratives tend to take. The message in the end is somewhat simple, didactic, and proscriptive—but uplifting in a sense. To the adolescent, the film says the world is hostile, but if you listen to adults and trust in your abilities, you can make it. As the general says, "Do exactly as I tell you and we will survive." It is this message which makes the film, while not exactly good, at least understandable. In the same vain as *Touching Spirit Bear*, *My Side of the Mountain*, and *Hatchet*, the film is intended to use the wilderness as an external symbol for the internal journey from childhood to adolescence. The message to adolescents who are watching? We've tried to protect you from the collapse of late capitalism by keeping you in the nursery (Žižek's denial phase), but we can't anymore—the world we have entered is too new, too alien for our collective adult wisdom to help you very much. Take what you can, whatever is useful, but you're going to have to fend for yourself in the wilderness. Though the general admonishes Kitai to do exactly as he says in order to survive, in the end, it is Kitai's own sense of what to do that allows him to survive.

Again, some might consider trying to shoehorn this film in with dystopian texts because it represents a kind of future that we don't want to see. Do we classify the film as dystopian? As ecocritical YA SF? Both? Consider for a moment the ways that many have struggled to create a definition that will work for the YA dystopian genre. Fredric Jameson, remember, attempted to define the dystopia as a text that occurs in what he calls the "near future" and deals with some kind of disaster (Jameson, "Seeds . . ." 56). A text that "tell[s] the story of an imminent disaster—ecology, overpopulation, plague, drought, the stray comet or nuclear accident—waiting to come to pass in our own near future, which is fast-forwarded in the time of the novel" (ibid. 56). Susan Stewart says of dystopian works that they are "cautionary tales set in a future with recognizable features" (159). In their excellent introduction to that same book, Carrie Hintz, Katherine R. Broad, and Balaka Basu say, "With its capacity to frighten and warn, dystopian writing engages with pressing global concerns: liberty and self-determination, environmental destruction and looming catastrophe, questions of identity, and the increasingly fragile boundaries between technology and the self" (1). Likewise, Ann M. M. Childs says, "Dystopian fiction written for young readers differs from adult dystopia in fundamental ways" (187). However, Childs points out that she feels there is hope of toppling the repressive regime in the YA dystopia, whether or not that toppling occurs within the text or at some later date, and none in the adult dystopia, that the dystopia intended for the adult audience focuses on a warning to prevent the future shown in the text, while the YA dystopia is about toppling an already-in-place repressive regime (Childs 187). The hope versus nihilism spectrum discussed earlier. While this is a difference I would agree with in many cases (certainly not all), this is not necessarily a *fundamental* difference. Certainly not one fundamental enough to label the two species of texts so drastically different. I believe that we can still draw what I would call fundamental *similarities* between YA and "adult" dystopian texts when it comes to definition.

A Final Thought

Thomas J. Morrissey says that "it is reasonable to assume that YA dystopian writers are hoping for [the same] efficacy; social activism is a viable and desirable reader response to utopian/dystopian

SF" (qtd. in Basu et al., 199–200). I agree. It is reasonable to assume that the writers intend for the works to cause these effects in their readers, and therefore we should be classifying these books based on those effects and then using them for those very effects.

Throughout this book, I have also offered up several other attempts people have made to define the genre. I have simultaneously attempted to deal with the problems we can run into when using the generic noun "dystopia" or the adjective "dystopian" rather than looking at attempts to define the genre because slippage between these things is apt to create a muddy mess for critics or anyone else to work with. Notice how so many of the attempts to define the genre have to swing quite wide in order to encompass all of the texts they see as dystopian (often because of the slippage that I just mentioned). What I suggest is that these definitions wind up being somewhat inaccurate because of the attempts to include such broad explanations, all of which come from the attempt to continue the use of the idea that dystopia is "a future that we don't like or want" (the definition rather than a genre classification). In itself, this is too wide a definition to be helpful. It means lumping texts into the same category that don't have anything to do with one another. It can also mean a mismatch between what we call dystopian in texts intended for adults versus those intended for a young audience. Consider for a moment the tendency of reviewers to call the film *Blade Runner* dystopian. Yet what does that film have in common with Orwell's *1984*? In that same vain, what does Anderson's *Feed* have in common with *Divergent*? As critics, we can stretch and find ways they are similar, but to a reader, do they truly share a common purpose/feeling? *Feed* and *Blade Runner* DO share commonality, though, if we place them both in the category of cyberpunk texts, as *1984* and *Divergent* DO share commonality if we place them in the category dystopian. While the contortions that critics must do to link some of these texts can often be brilliant, they are contortions nevertheless.[9]

The problem, if, indeed, you agree with me that there is one, with coming to understand these works is still one of genre. If we are still lumping apocalyptic science fiction and ecocritical science fiction in with politically based dystopian works, then the water is still too muddy to see. *Feed* by M. T. Anderson is a text I routinely see named "dystopian," for instance. However, from the point of view of someone studying science fiction, that text clearly participates in the tradition called cyberpunk (or, to be even more precise, post-cyberpunk). It has much more in common with a film like *Johnny Mnemonic* than it has to do with *The Hunger Games*. This, again, is in no way a judgment on the novel's quality, but is, instead, an attempt to make sure we are looking at the work through the lens of other works like it. Consider for a moment an article published on the culture website Vulture.com in August of 2017. They published a list of what they called the "100 Great Works of Dystopian Fiction." On that list they make the case for books like H. G. Well's *The Time Machine* and Rand's *Atlas Shrugged* to be considered dystopian works. Admittedly, Vulture is not an academic site, but these kinds of lists crop up quite often on the net. This means that there seems to be a lack of clear definition.

I realize that there will be resistance to my attempt to place things into what could easily be seen as rigid categories. I'm very aware of Carl Freedman's insistence that science fiction is more of a mode of writing that a writer chooses to use in combination of other modes than a stable genre, as I've said.[10] With that in mind, all of these classifications can be seen as modes, as ways to approach an intended set of themes, thereby rendering any attempt to place a text definitively in any one particular category difficult to say the least. However, as I've also suggested, sorting them is part of our job as critics, teachers, and scholars. We do this not to attempt to rank the works' quality, but instead to make sure that when we suggest these works or assign them, we know what effect they are producing in the reader. Even Freedman points out that a work will almost always have one overarching mode in which it is working, and very often a clear subgenre.

I should note, too, that in making these distinctions, I am not attempting some act of genre protectionism. As I've stated, I believe that these divisions are useful in helping us understand ways of deploying these texts in various spaces such as classrooms, not as ways of keeping any particular genre "pure."

At first glance, it may seem as though I am championing the didactic impulse so many writers have when writing for young people, or, worse, that I applaud those who police the written work that young people may have access to based solely on whether or not it teaches the reader something (usually something that aligns with the gatekeeper's own ideological agenda). Trust me when I say that nothing could be further from my goal. If we examine use value, we are not somehow abandoning other aspects of any given text in question. I still firmly believe that young people should have a variety of texts available to them and that they should be allowed to choose freely among those texts based on their own criteria, their own wishes. I am simply suggesting that for the purposes of critique, there exist differences in why a young person might choose dystopian work over science fiction (or vice versa), and that reason might be because of the work that genre is doing on them consciously or subconsciously.[11] We might also use these divisions to study that very didactic impulse I mentioned earlier by asking the question, "why does X seem to prefer assigning texts in this genre over that one in their class?"

Finally, I must point out that it is not the case that the theory I have presented here is *only* present in dystopian literature. Or that science fiction does not have its own complex patterns of identity formation and policing present. What I offer here, as I've said, is merely the beginnings of a way to differentiate the two by looking at the work that they do so that we can more clearly look at what effects these texts have on their readers.

I've loved science fiction my whole life. Dystopian literature came into my life much later, but inspired in me no less love than science fiction did. Once I started studying young adult literature, especially dystopian literature for young adults, I saw that so many theorists working in science fiction for young adults and dystopian YA are often trying to reinvent the wheel by coming up with new theories for these genres. While those theories are often brilliant, there is usually someone studying dystopian literature intended for adults and science fiction that isn't specifically earmarked for a YA audience who has some thoughts on the subject already. In other words, I saw that perhaps my contribution could be to bring these discourses together and have them start talking to one another.

My goal in writing this book was to point out that the study of science fiction and the study of dystopian literature are both longstanding traditions. They have their own terminologies, ideologies, histories, and so on. In studying dystopian literature for young adults, rather than reinventing the wheel with the requisite stumbles such an undertaking involves, we as scholars should avail ourselves of the already-existing critical discourses. When we do, we see that dystopian YA is not some new thing that defies previous definition, but instead participates in (and, simultaneously, does not participate in other) long-standing traditions. Once we understand the way these texts participate in and/or resist those earlier traditions, we are in a much better place to then use these texts in ways that benefit young people most. My sincere hope is that this book is a helpful jumping-off point for study of these genres, especially in drilling down into the mass of texts that were produced during the time of the trend and perhaps did not receive as much critical attention as they deserved because of the sheer volume of works that were appearing at the time. I also hope that the theory presented here can be helpfully combined with other theories to form even more useful lenses for that examination. Whether the texts are attempting to explore the ways that humans interact with the o/Other or examine the ways that the power of the Order creates subjectivity, taking the time to survey how these texts affect young people is a vitally important enterprise.

NOTES

Introduction

1. Here I am referring to the Althusserian concepts of the Ideological State Apparatus and the Repressive State Apparatus, which I will further expand and explore in chapter 1.

2. Let me state, for the record, that I do not believe this to be somehow depriving them of "greater literature" in any way; I am merely noticing a trend, and using that trend as a place to center the observation that begins my conversation.

3. The main exception being, of course, the sections set aside for manga, which are often, though not always, near those set aside for young adult literature.

Chapter 1. Interpellation, Identification, and the Boundary between Self and o/Other

1. Even while saying this, I am also aware of Roberta Trites's assertion that another purpose for YA literature of any kind is the very formation of the adolescent's subjectivity. I am also aware of Adorno's point that any object of mass or popular culture, such as mainstream YA literature, functions to legitimize dominant ideology.

2. It is important to acknowledge that Foucault himself has discouraged the conflation of his theories, based on the effects of power on the body, with Althusser's sense of state apparatuses. He says, "One of the first things that has to be understood is that power isn't localized in the State apparatus and that nothing in society will be changed if the mechanisms of power that function outside, below

and alongside the state apparatuses, on a much more minute and everyday level, are not also changed" (*Power/Knowledge*, 60). He says he feels that our focus should be more on "strategic apparatus" (102). We should be looking at the strategies and tactics in which power is enacted, he feels. If there is hope for intervention, it comes from there.

3. As Lacan points out, the very structure of the unconscious itself is like a language.

4. Another way we might see the Other is that which is outside the realm of language and thought—that space of radical alterity, a place where the Symbolic order breaks down in the face of the Real. It is Other because it is outside the realm of the possible, ontologically, because it is outside of the realm of language.

5. It should be noted that Toumayan asserts that we must disavow any attempt to summarize Levinas's work as reductive, and therefore against the very principles that Levinas posits. An interesting argument, if unconvincing (171–73).

6. Coats also points out her surprise that Kristeva didn't link the idea of the adolescent to the concept of the abject.

7. As I will soon show, cognitive estrangement is facilitated by the coding of the other.

Chapter 2. "The Electric Boy Grows Up": Science Fiction for a Young Adult Audience

1. Here I am appropriating Francis J. Molson's 1981 adaptation of Francis Hodgson Burnett's 1892 term for her son. For more, see his article, "Writing for the 'Electric Boy': Notes on the Origins of Children's SF."

2. Here, I'm referring back to the self/other binary that begins at the time of the mirror stage. Please refer back to the section in chapter 1 on Lacanian subject formation.

3. "Nodal point" is the Ernesto Laclau/Chantal Mouffe term for areas of contemporary ideology where several strands intersect and overlap to form somewhat stable identifications in a Burkean sense. See *Hegemony and Socialist Strategy: Towards a Radical Democratic Politics* (London: Verso, 1985).

4. It should be noted that Jameson means what we might refer to as sword-and-sorcery when he refers to "fantasy" and not the more inclusive term that we use in studying children's literature.

5. Though my purpose in this chapter is not to explore the origins of science fiction, there are some excellent books on the subject available such as Brian Stableford's *Scientific Romance in Britain 1890–1950*; Darko Suvin's *Victorian Science Fiction in the UK: The Discourses of Knowledge and of Power*; and Martin Willis's

Mesmerists, Monsters and Machines: The Science Fiction and the Cultures of Science in the Nineteenth Century.

6. I am aware that the term "fathers" of the field excludes Mary Shelley, whose works predate Jules Verne by nearly sixty years, and is sexist. I use it here because this is the common, shared terminology.

7. Cyberpunk is generally thought of as having begun with the 1982 film *Blade Runner* and William Gibson's 1984 novel *Neuromancer*.

8. Here I'm thinking of M. T. Anderson's *Feed*, a very good example of a YA post-cyberpunk novel.

9. Consider the James Bond film series: gadgetry is a primary characteristic of the films, and yet they tend to uphold status quo rather than question it. This is why they are not science fiction.

10. Here I am invoking Bahktin's sense of a double-voiced discourse when I say "dialogic." Science fiction is by its very nature an intersecting node of ideolects bent toward interrogation of monologic discourse. For more on this, see Freedman.

11. As I will soon show, cognitive estrangement is facilitated by the coding of the other.

12. Coats's concept of the adolescent as abject from the social body is particularly apt here. In this case, the social body is the high school Jeremy attends.

13. Something very interesting to me is that Vizzini here shows that the computer doesn't speak, but interrupts directly into the narration—notice there are no quotation marks around the computer's Keanu Reeves–like voice. Its voice not only occurs in Jeremy's head, but in the same space as Jeremy's narration-thought itself. The computer becomes a co-narrator. Gennette might call this pseudo-metalepsis into the intradiegetic narration.

14. An important point Freedman makes is that like all genres of fiction, science fictional generic tendencies are only one small part of the interplay of tendencies that make up any given SF text. He points out that in many novels considered non-science fiction by the canon, SF is a tendency they, too, show, but to a much lesser degree than texts which we call "science fiction."

15. I'm thinking here of such titles as *Journey to the Haunted Planet* by A. J. Wood and *Eager* by Helen Fox, respectively.

16. Here I'm thinking of *My Teacher Is an Alien* by Bruce Coveille as well as others that use the same trope.

17. Here I'm thinking specifically of the short story "Robbie" by Isaac Asimov, in which a family buys a robot for their home, but when the young daughter becomes too attached and rejects what the parents see as "normal" social bonding with other children, they get rid of the robot, causing great emotional distress to the daughter. See also Gary Wolfe's excellent section on the robot as metaphor in *The Known and the Unknown*.

18. In Rosenbaum's novel, this process of vitrification is the novum.

19. Of course, the referent is also *Sleeping Beauty*. In that sense, the protagonist's gender is not a new twist on the trope. However, for the field of dystopian or science fiction literature, the protagonist is more often a male awakened in the future than a female. See note 20.

20. See Edward Bellamy's *Looking Backward*, William Morris's *News from Nowhere*, or Philip Francis Nowlan's *Armageddon 2419 AD*, for more of this trope as a way of exploring utopia/dystopia.

21. "Skinner" is a slur for those who have had their consciousness downloaded into mech bodies.

Chapter 3. "The Treatment for Stirrings": Dystopian Literature for Adolescents

1. I believe that there is simply not enough space in one chapter to consider the unique concerns of film as well as the theoretical perspectives on dystopian films and novels.

2. I do not intend this move as a dismissal of the decades of work that have gone on in utopian studies, nor do I see flaw in the conscientious parsing of terms. Instead, I intend this as a move designed to keep this book's initial goal clear. In chapter 2, for instance, I did not stop to parse through the difference between time-travel science fiction and space opera; likewise, I do not intend for this chapter to get bogged down in attempting to examine the gradations of the various views on differing modes of utopian thought. For more on that, I recommend Thomas Moylan's book, *Scraps of the Untainted Sky*.

3. Here, they are specifically speaking of the novel *The True Story of Hansel and Gretel* as well as the film *Spirited Away*, neither of which I would put into the category of critical dystopia as I define it.

4. Here I want to make sure we understand that while I believe there is a difference between dystopian writing for children and dystopian writing for young adults, I believe Sambell is folding the two together in this statement. I use her statement as a way of thinking about the YA dystopian novel.

5. See "Introduction: Zamyatin and the Persian Rooster" in *We*, trans. Clarence Brown. (New York: Penguin, 1993).

6. Here, I'm thinking of Shelley's *The Last Man* as an early example of the post-disaster narrative, and Sir Thomas More's classic *Utopia* as the ultimate pattern for the traveling-to-utopia pattern.

7. I will discuss DuPrau's novel later in this chapter, while my analysis of Westerfeld's work will form the bulk of chapter 5.

8. For more on this, see such works as Frank Black's *IBM and the Holocaust: The Strategic Alliance between Nazi Germany and America's Most Powerful Corporation* (New York: Crown, 2001).

9. This novel functions as a young adult dystopian narrative, even though later novels in the series are actually post-disaster narratives.

10. This is much like the structure of *The Giver*, which I will discuss later in this chapter. In that novel, too, children are sent into the workforce at twelve. I believe that this says a lot about our conceptions of childhood as protected space, and how closely that is tied with the onset of puberty; that is, that the adolescent, even at the onset, is now ready to join the workforce and be constructed as a "worker" as part of their new subjectivity within the community structure.

11. See Coats, 142–43, and Trites, xi.

12. As distasteful as that sounds, it pales in comparison to the actual description of an unwinding which occurs near the end of the novel.

13. For more on this, please see chapter 5 in *Archaeologies of the Future*.

14. Here, I'm thinking about McArthy's *The Road*, where both film and novel get called dystopian on a regular basis.

15. Examples include Atwood's *The Handmaid's Tale*, and, in children's/YA literature, the sequels to Jeanne DuPrau's *The City of Ember*, which we will discuss later in this chapter.

16. I'm referring to a case such as Rodman Philbrick's *The Last Book in the Universe*, which has been called dystopian but is actually more picaresque than anything else—it is much more science fiction than dystopian literature, but because it involves several scenes of decayed urban sprawl, it gets called dystopian when perhaps dystopic is a better term.

17. Of course, in the later novel *The Messenger*, Jonas (or at least a remarkably Jonas-like character) does appear. However, I wish to confine my examination of *The Giver* to the text itself.

Chapter 4. "Teaching the Fantastic": Using Science Fiction and Dystopian Texts in the Classroom

1. It is important to note that while I have worked to point out the differences between the two genres of dystopian literature for young adults and science fiction for that same group, many who have published on teaching do not make this distinction. Dystopian texts regularly appear on the reading lists for classes that are called science fiction.

2. Rodden is paraphrasing Albert B. Friedman, "The Literary Experiences of High School Seniors and College Freshmen," *English Journal* 44 (1955): 420–26.

3. Rodden is pulling from G. Yarlott and W. S. Harpin, "1000 Responses to English Literature (2)," *Educational Research* 13 (February 1971): 90–96.

4. See Patrick Parrinder, *Science Fiction: Its Criticism and Its Teaching* (London: Methuen, 1980) and/or Jack Williamson, *Teaching Science Fiction: Education for Tomorrow* (Philadelphia: Owlswick Press, 1980).

5. For a transcription of that conversation, see John Woodcock, Gregory Benford, Samuel Delany, Robert Scholes, and Alan J. Friedman, "Teaching Science Fiction: Unique Challenges (Proceedings of the MLA Special Session, New York, December 1978)," *Science Fiction Studies* 6.3 (1979): 249–62.

6. Issues of how to define an SF canon have also arisen, though I will not be examining that issue here. Jack Williamson has said, however: "Though critics have been trying to select a canon, the lists of books in use still vary vastly. Tabulating nearly eighty reading lists, a few years ago, I found some 300 titles named, half of them only once. Even the most popular were used in less than half the classes. That was before the flood of special classroom anthologies and before the mass publishers began trying to reach the schools, but the results may still be suggestive" (16).

7. Examples of the former would include articles such as Myra Barnes, "Using Science Fiction to Teach Linguistics," from *College Composition and Communication* 26.4 (1975); E. E. Nunan and David Homer, "Science, Science Fiction, and a Radical Science Education," in *Science Fiction Studies* 24.8 (1981): 311–30; or Michael Barnett et al.'s fascinating "The Impact of Science Fiction Film on Student Understanding of Science," from *Journal of Science Education and Technology* 15.2 (2006): 179–91.

8. She begins her argument with the X-Men, which I view as much more a superhero genre story than a science fiction one.

9. This is certainly in line with Maria Nikolajeva's assertion in *Power, Voice, and Subjectivity in Literature for Young Readers*, that "many critics have repeatedly pointed out, children's literature is utopian by nature. As a consequence, children's fiction maintains myth of a happy and innocent childhood, apparently based on adult writers' nostalgic memories and bitter insights about the impossibility of returning to the childhood idyll" (73).

10. Even as I write that, I am aware of the unfortunate rise in censorship through the rhetoric of comfort in the contemporary secondary and even postsecondary classroom. "That makes me uncomfortable" seems to be a rallying cry for students (often being egged on by political rhetoric) to call for substitution of one text for another or, as is more often the case, the removal of a text from a course altogether.

11. Here she is quoting the work of Romøren and Stephens from 2002 titled, "Representing Masculinities in Norwegian and Australian Young Adult Fiction: A Comparative Study."

12. As initially described by Carol Gilligan in 1982's *In a Different Voice*.

13. This, of course, begs the question many feminist scholars have asked of the series, namely, "why does she *have* to wind up with anybody?" It is a valid question. I don't intend my use of Littman's work to negate such a question, merely to elaborate on one half of that equation.

14. This is especially true considering the "War on Terror" is still ongoing and shows no sign of ending any time soon.

15. Indeed, the very crux of their argument in this article is the sorting hat test that creates one of the major themes of the Harry Potter series.

16. While I contest one of those categories, the environmental catastrophe, the other two are sound descriptions of what I would call dystopian. As we've discussed previously, this category is the result of the definitional slippage between ecocritical works and dystopian works.

17. As an interesting side note, in one class I was teaching, the students and I read Nicholas Carr's excellent book, 2010's *The Shallows: What the Internet Is Doing to Our Brains*. In the book, Carr explores the many ways that the Internet has changed us socially, physiologically, and neurologically. Throughout our discussions, students were able to identify with the most apocalyptic of Carr's assertions/predictions, but interestingly enough indicated time and time again that they had no intention of changing their behavior.

18. Though I do take Carter F. Hanson's point that not *all* YA dystopian fiction deals with sociopolitical critique in more than a superficial way. For more on this, see his 2015 article, "Postmodernity and Digital Memory Versus Human Remembering in M. T. Anderson's *Feed*"—though he and I would disagree on whether or not *Feed* is, indeed, YA dystopian fiction or YA post-cyberpunk, hence the reason that it "differs strikingly from most young adult dystopian fictions" (259).

19. This concept echoes through many classic dystopian texts, including Huxley's *Brave New World*, and even much more recent examples such as the 2002 film *Equilibrium*.

Chapter 5. "Signs of Life": Considerations for the Future of the Genres and Their Critique

1. Though, it could also be said that Chelsom's film is a less-mystical, more twenty-first-century YA homage to Heinlein's 1961 classic novel, *Stranger in a Strange Land*.

2. Here I'm talking about *Star Trek: Discovery* and *The Orville*, respectively.

3. 2012's *Prometheus*, 2017's *Alien: Covenant* and 2017's *Blade Runner 2049*, respectively.

4. Indeed, given the highly contentious results of the 2016 presidential election in America, I suspect there will be a renewed interest in these texts and a wave of

new titles starting in 2017 (the earliest new dystopian texts might arrive in print). Indeed, if we can extrapolate from that, we might take the prevalence of articles regarding dystopian works popping up in venues that don't traditionally cover literature as a sign of some sort. Consider Wendy Fawthrop's September 5, 2017, article in the *Orange County Register* titled "Are Dystopian Novels a Call to Action for Millennials?" in which a CSUF student sees a brave new world where a Cal State Fullerton student's paper regarding the connection between dystopian works and millennial activism is covered.

    5. *Children's Literature*, volume 44, 2016.

    6. From *Extrapolation*, volume 57, numbers 1 and 2, 2016.

    7. Much of this still survives in the stereotypical high school experience of the twenty-first century. I point out specifically "of the 20th century" because many of the writers currently creating YA dystopian works are products of that experience and not the newer experience, which, in some ways, their works are helping to define/change.

    8. To briefly recap, consider that James Patterson's 2011 novel, *Middle School: The Worst Years of My Life* (and the 2016 film based on it), is very much a dystopian novel with a contemporary, non-sci-fi setting.

    9. Here, I'm thinking of work like Bridgitte Barclay's "Perpetually Waving to an Unseen Crowd" from *Female Rebellion in Young Adult Dystopian Fiction*. She makes an excellent case for thinking of Libba Bray's novel, *Beauty Queens*, as dystopian in that essay. While I agree that much of Western civilization has functioned like a dystopian society for women and girls, the novel itself shares very little in common with what we might think of as the staples of the dystopian genre, be it written for adolescents or for adults.

    10. Again, see Carl Freedman's excellent *Critical Theory and Science Fiction*.

    11. Of course, there is more than a little irony, as pointed out by more than one standup comedian, in the fact that so much of dystopian work is predicated on the premise of warning the reader that some fictionalized totalitarian regime has gained/is gaining access to their private lives via advances in technology and yet all our newest "smart" technology involves devices that are constantly recording us, or that we assist such regimes with each Facebook status update but also by tagging each picture we post on Instagram with the identities of those around us.

BIBLIOGRAPHY

Agamben, Giorgio. *Homo Sacer: Sovereign Power and Bare Life*. Stanford, CA: Stanford UP, 1998.
Alexander, Jonathan, and Rebecca Black. "The Darker Side of the Sorting Hat: Representations of Educational Testing in Dystopian Young Adult Fiction." *Children's Literature* 43 (2015): 208–34.
Althusser, Louis. "Ideology and Ideological State Apparatuses." *Lenin and Philosophy and Other Essays*. Trans. Ben Brewster. New York: New York Monthly Review P, 2001. 85–126.
Ames, Melissa A. "Engaging 'Apolitical' Adolescents: Analyzing the Popularity and Educational Potential of Dystopian Literature Post-9/11." *Faculty Research & Creative Activity*. Paper 11. 2013. http://thekeep.eiu.edu/eng_fac/11.08/2017.
Ames, Mildred. *Anna to the Infinite Power*. New York: Scholastic, 1981.
Anderson, Erland. "Three Cheers for Science Fiction." *College Composition and Communication* 25.2 (1974): 203–5.
Asimov, Isaac. "Introduction: The First Century of Science Fiction." *Isaac Asimov Presents the Best Science Fiction of the 19th Century*. Ed. Isaac Asimov, Charles G. Waugh, and Martin Greenberg. New York: Beaufort Books, 1981. 9–12.
Baccolini, Rafaella. "The Persistence of Hope in Dystopian Science Fiction." *PMLA* 119.3 (2004): 518–21.
Bartter, Martha. "Young Adults, Science Fiction and War." *Young Adult Science Fiction*. Ed. C. W. Sullivan III. Westport, CT: Greenwood, 1999. 131–46.
Basu, Balaka, Katherine R. Broad, and Carrie Hintz. "Introduction." *Contemporary Dystopian Fiction for Young Adults*. Ed. Balaka Basu, Katherine R. Broad, and Carrie Hintz. New York: Routledge, 2013. 1–15.
Baudrillard, Jean. *Simulacra and Simulation*. Ann Arbor: U of Michigan P, 1994.

Beebee, Thomas O. *The Ideology of Genre: A Comparative Study of Generic Instability*. University Park: Pennsylvania State UP, 1994.
Bixler, Andrea. "Teaching Evolution with the Aid of Science Fiction." *American Biology Teacher* 69.6 (2007): 337–40.
Booker, M. Keith. *The Dystopian Impulse in Modern Literature: Fiction as Social Criticism*. Westport, CT: Greenwood, 1994.
Booker, M. Keith. *Dystopian Literature: A Theory and Research Guide*. Westport, CT: Greenwood, 1994.
"Books R4 Teens." College of Education, University of Texas at Austin. 2005. http://www.edb.utexas.edu/resources/booksR4teens/book_reviews/book_reviews.php?book_id=4 (accessed August 1, 2009).
Bracher, Mark. "Identity and Desire in the Classroom." *Pedagogical Desire: Authority, Seduction, Transference, and the Question of Ethics*. Ed. Jan Jagodzinski. Santa Barbara, CA: Greenwood, 2002. 93–121.
Bradford, Clare, Kerry Mallan, John Stephens, and Robyn McCallum. *New World Orders in Contemporary Children's Literature: Utopian Transformations*. New York: Palgrave, 2008.
Bullen, Elizabeth, and Elizabeth Parsons. "Dystopian Visions of Global Capitalism: Philip Reeve's *Mortal Engines* and M. T. Anderson's *Feed*." *Children's Literature in Education* 38.2 (2007): 127–39.
Burke, Kenneth. *A Rhetoric of Motives*. 1950. Berkeley: U of California P, 1969.
Calkins, Elizabeth, and Barry McGhan. "Science Fiction in the High School." *Teaching Science Fiction: Education for Tomorrow*. Ed. Jack Williamson. Philadelphia: Owlswick Press, 1980. 82–96.
Callinicos, Alex. *Althusser's Marxism*. London: Pluto, 1976.
Carter, C. Allen. *Kenneth Burke and the Scapegoat Process*. Norman: U of Oklahoma P, 1996.
Childs, Ann M. M. "Chapter 11: The Incompatibility of Female Friendships and Rebellion." *Female Rebellion in Young Adult Dystopian Fiction*. Ed. Sara K. Day, Miranda A. Green-Barteet, and Amy L. Montz. New York: Routledge, 2014. 187–201.
Cixous, Hélène, and Catherine Clément. *The Newly Born Woman*. Trans. Betsy Wing. 1975. Minneapolis: U of Minnesota P, 1986.
Clarke, Simon. "Althusserian Marxism." *One-Dimensional Marxism: Althusser and the Politics of Culture*. London: Allison and Busby, 1980. 7–102.
Coats, Karen. *Looking Glasses and Neverlands: Lacan, Desire and Subjectivity in Children's Literature*. Iowa City: U of Iowa P, 2004.
Cohn, Dorrit. "Optics and Power in the Novel." *New Literary History* 26.1 (1995): 3–20.
Couzelis, Mary J. "Chapter Eight: The Future Is Pale: Race in Contemporary Young Adult Dystopian Novels." *Contemporary Dystopian Fiction for Young*

Adults. Ed. Balaka Basu, Katherine R. Broad, and Carrie Hintz. New York: Routledge, 2013. 131–44.

Dashner, James. *The Maze Runner*. New York: Delacorte, 2009.

"The Day the Earth Stood Still." Performers: Michael Rennie, Patricia Neal. Director: Robert Wise. 20th Century Fox. 1951.

de la Durantaye, Leland. *Giorgio Agamben: A Critical Introduction*. Stanford: Stanford UP, 2009.

Donawerth, Jane. "Teaching Science Fiction by Women." *English Journal* 79.3 (1990): 39–46.

Dubrow, Heather. *Genre*. New York: Methuen, 1982.

Duff, David. "Introduction." *Modern Genre Theory*. Ed. David Duff. Harlow, UK: Pearson Longman, 2000. 1–24.

DuPrau, Jeanne. *The City of Ember*. New York: Random House, 2003.

Elliot, Amy. "Power in Our Words: Finding Community and Mitigating Trauma in James Dashner's *The Maze Runner*." *Children's Literature Association Quarterly* 40.2 (2015): 179–99.

Engdahl, Sylvia. *Enchantress from the Stars*. 1970. New York: Collier, 1989.

Foucault, Michel. Discipline and Punish: The Birth of the Prison. 2nd ed. New York: Vintage, 1995.

Foucault, Michel. *Power/Knowledge: Selected Interviews and Other Writings 1972–1977*. Ed. Colin Gordon. New York: Pantheon, 1980.

Freedman, Carl. *Critical Theory and Science Fiction*. London: Wesleyan UP, 2000.

Freedman, Kerry. "An Aesthetic of Horror in Education: Schools as Dystopian Environments." *Dystopia and Education: Insights into Theory, Praxis, and Policy in an Age of Utopia-Gone-Wrong*. Ed. Jessica A. Heybach and Eric C. Sheffield. Charlotte, NC: Information Age Publishing, 2013. 3–13.

Freire, Paulo. *Pedagogy of the Oppressed*. 1970. New York: Continuum, 1996.

Godzich, Wlad. "Foreword: The Further Possibility of Knowledge." *Heterologies: Discourses on the Other*. Trans. Brian Massumi. Minneapolis: U of Minnesota P, 1986. vii–xxi.

Gordon, Joan. "Utopia, Genocide and the Other." *Edging into the Future: Science Fiction and Contemporary Cultural Transformation*. Ed. Veronica Hollinger and Joan Gordon. Philadelphia: U of Pennsylvania P, 2002. 205–16.

Gordon, Joan, and Veronica Hollinger. "Introduction." *Edging into the Future: Science Fiction and Contemporary Cultural Transformation*. Ed. Veronica Hollinger and Joan Gordon. Philadelphia: U of Pennsylvania P, 2002. 1–8.

Gordon, Neve. "Foucault's Subject: An Ontological Reading." *Polity* 31.3 (1999): 395–414.

Gunn, James. *Inside Science Fiction: Essays on Fantastic Literature*. San Bernardino, CA: Borgo Press, 1992.

Gunn, James. "Teaching Science Fiction." *Science Fiction Studies* 23.3 (1996): 377–84.
Haddix, Margaret Peterson. *Among the Hidden*. New York: Simon and Schuster, 1998.
Harris-Fain, Darren. *Understanding Contemporary American Science Fiction: The Age of Maturity, 1970–2000*. Columbia: U of South Carolina P, 2005.
Hatch, Rachel. "Professor: Divergent movie hits dystopian nerve with Teens." *STATEside's Office Hours Series*. Illinois State University. March 11, 2014. https://news.illinoisstate.edu/2014/03/professor-divergent-movie-hits-dystopian-nerve-teens/ (accessed August 2016).
Hatty, Suzanne E. *Masculinities, Violence and Culture*. Thousand Oaks, CA: Sage, 2000.
Heller, Kevin Jon. "Subjectification and Resistance in Foucault." *SubStance* 25.1, Issue 79 (1996): 78–110.
Hintz, Carrie, and Elaine Ostry. "Introduction." *Utopian and Dystopian Writing for Children and Young Adults*. Ed. Carrie Hintz and Elaine Ostry. New York: Taylor and Francis Books, 2003. 1–22.
Hollindale, Peter. *Signs of Childness in Children's Books*. Stroud, England: Thimble, 1997.
hooks, bell. *Teaching to Transgress: Education and the Practice of Freedom*. New York: Routledge, 1994.
Jameson, Fredric. *Archaeologies of the Future: The Desire Called Utopia and Other Science Fictions*. London: Verso, 2005.
Jameson, Fredric. *The Seeds of Time*. New York: Columbia University Press. 1994.
Lawrence, Louise. *Dream-Weaver*. New York: Clarion, 1996.
Le Guin, Ursala. "On Teaching Science Fiction." *Teaching Science Fiction: Education for Tomorrow*. Ed. Jack Williamson. Philadelphia: Owlswick Press, 1980. 21–25.
Littman, Sarah Darer. "The Politics of Mockingjay." *The Girl Who Was on Fire*. Ed. Leah Wilson. Dallas, TX: Smart Pop, 2010. 163–78.
Longyear, Barry. "Science Fiction and the Primary School." *Teaching Science Fiction: Education for Tomorrow*. Ed. Jack Williamson. Philadelphia: Owlswick Press, 1980. 75–81.
Lovell, Terry. "The Social Relations of Cultural Production: Absent Centre of a New Discourse." *One-Dimensional Marxism: Althusser and the Politics of Culture*. London: Allison and Busby, 1980. 232–56.
Lowry, Lois. *The Giver*. New York: Delacourte, 1993.
McDonnell, Kevin, and Kevin Robins. "Marxist Cultural Theory: The Althusserian Smokescreen." *One-Dimensional Marxism: Althusser and the Politics of Culture*. London: Allison and Busby, 1980. 157–231.
McKay, George. "Metapropaganda: Self-Reading Dystopian Fiction: Burdekin's Swastika Night and Orwell's Nineteen Eighty-Four." *Science Fiction Studies* 21.3 (1994): 302–14.

Mendlesohn, Farah. "Is There Any Such Thing as Children's Science Fiction?: A Position Piece." *The Lion and the Unicorn* 28 (2004): 284–313.

Molson, Francis J. "Writing for the 'Electric Boy': Notes on the Origins of Children's SF." *Children's Literature Association Quarterly* 5.4 (1981): 9–12.

Molson, Francis J. "American Technological Fiction for Youth: 1900–1940." *Young Adult Science Fiction*. Ed. C. W. Sullivan III. Westport, CT: Greenwood, 1999. 7–20.

Montag, Warren. "'The Soul Is the Prison of the Body': Althusser and Foucault, 1970–1975." *Yale French Studies* 88 (1995): 53–77.

Mosley, Walter. *47*. New York: Little, Brown and Company, 2005.

Moylan, Tom. *Scraps of the Untainted Sky: Science Fiction, Utopia, Dystopia*. Boulder, CO: Westview, 2000.

Nodelman, Perry. "Futurism in Young Adult Science Fiction." *Children's Literature Review* 116 (2006): 169–76.

"100 Great Works of Dystopian Fiction: Tales about a World Gone Wrong." *Vulture.com*. August 3, 2017. www.vulture.com/article/best-dystopian-books.html.

Orwell, George. *1984*. 1949. New York: Plume, 1983.

Ostry, Elaine. "'Is He Still Human? Are You?': Young Adult Science Fiction in the Posthuman Age." *The Lion and the Unicorn* 28 (2004): 222–46.

Parrinder, Patrick. *Science Fiction: Its Criticism and Its Teaching*. London: Methuen, 1980.

Plank, Robert. "Science Fiction and Psychology." *Teaching Science Fiction: Education for Tomorrow*. Ed. Jack Williamson. Philadelphia: Owlswick Press, 1980. 157–67.

Ratcliffe, Krista. *Rhetorical Listening: Identification, Gender, Whiteness*. Carbondale: Southern Illinois UP, 2005.

Reid, Suzanne Elizabeth. *Presenting Young Adult Science Fiction*. New York: Simon and Schuster, 1998.

Reynolds, Kimberley. *Radical Children's Literature: Future Visions and Aesthetic Transformations in Juvenile Fiction*. New York: Palgrave, 2007.

Roberts, Adam. *Science Fiction*. London: Routledge, 2000.

Roberts, Thomas J. "Science Fiction and the Adolescent." *Children's Literature* 2 (1973): 87–91.

Rodden, John. "Canon-Formation, Pedagogy: George Orwell in the Classroom." *College English* 53.5 (1991): 503–30.

Roemer, Kenneth M. "Utopian Literature, Empowering Students, and Gender Awareness." *Science Fiction Studies* 23.3 (1996): 393–405.

Rosenbaum, Bev Katz. *I Was a Teenage Popsicle*. New York: Berkely Publishing Group, 2006.

Rybakova, Katie, and Rikki Roccanti. "Connecting the Canon to Current Young Adult Literature." *American Secondary Education* 44.2 (2016): 31–45.

Sagan, Carl. "Preface." *Teaching Science Fiction: Education for Tomorrow.* Ed. Jack Williamson. Philadelphia: Owlswick Press, 1980. 1–8.

Sambell, Kay. "Presenting the Case for Social Change: The Creative Dilemma of Dystopian Writing for Children." *Utopian and Dystopian Writing for Children and Young Adults.* Ed. Carrie Hintz and Elaine Ostry. New York: Taylor and Francis Books, 2003. 163–78.

Sambell, Kay. "Carnivalizing the Future: A New Approach to Theorizing Childhood and Adulthood in Science Fiction for Young Readers." *The Lion and the Unicorn* 28 (2004): 247–67.

Samuelson, Dave, Gary Goshgarian, and Dennis Livingston. "Three Syllabi." *Teaching Science Fiction: Education for Tomorrow.* Ed. Jack Williamson. Philadelphia: Owlswick Press, 1980. 194–202.

Sands, Karen, and Marietta Frank. *Back in the Spaceship Again: Juvenile Science Fiction Series since 1945.* Westport, CT: Greenwood, 1999.

Sargent, Lymon Tower. "Afterword." *Utopian and Dystopian Writing for Children and Young Adults.* Ed. Carrie Hintz and Elaine Ostry. New York: Taylor and Francis Books, 2003. 232–34.

Scholes, Robert. *Structural Fabulation: An Essay on the Fiction of the Future.* Notre Dame, IN: U of Notre Dame P, 1975.

Seymour, Jessica. "'Murder Me . . . Become a Man': Establishing the Masculine Care Circle in Young Adult Dystopia." *Reading Psychology* 37 (2015): 627–49.

Shusterman, Neal. *Unwind.* New York: Simon and Schuster, 2007.

Steele, Meili. *Theorizing Textual Subjects.* New York: Cambridge UP, 1997.

Steward, Susan Louise. "Chapter Ten: Dystopian Sacrifice, Scapegoats, and Neal Shusterman's Unwind." *Contemporary Dystopian Fiction for Young Adults.* Ed. Balaka Basu, Katherine R. Broad, and Carrie Hintz. New York: Routledge, 2013. 159–73.

Strasser, Todd. *The Wave.* New York: Laurel-Leaf, 1981.

Sullivan, C. W., III. "Introduction." *Young Adult Science Fiction.* Ed. C. W. Sullivan III. Westport, CT: Greenwood, 1999. 1–3.

Sullivan, C. W., III. "American Young Adult Science Fiction since 1947." *Young Adult Science Fiction.* Ed. C. W. Sullivan III. Westport, CT: Greenwood, 1999. 21–35.

Svilpis, Jānis. "Authority, Autonomy, and Adventure in Juvenile Science Fiction." *Children's Literature Association Quarterly* 8.3 (1983): 22–26.

THX 1138. Performers: Robert Duvall, Donald Pleasence. Director: George Lucas. American Zoetrope. 2004.

Todorov, Tzvetan. "The Origin of Genres." Ed. David Duff. *Modern Genre Theory.* Harlow, UK: Pearson Longman, 2000. 193–209.

Toumayan, Alain P. *Encountering the Other: The Artwork and the Problem of Difference in Blanchot and Levinas.* Pittsburgh, PA: Duquesne UP, 2004.

Trites, Roberta Seelinger. Dis*turbing the Universe: Power and Repression in Adolescent Literature*. Iowa City: U of Iowa P, 2000.
Vighi, Fabio, and Heiko Feldner. *Žižek: Beyond Foucault*. New York: Palgrave, 2007.
Vizzini, Ned. Be *More Chill*. New York: Hyperion, 2004.
Warrick, Patricia. "Images of the Man-Machine." *Many Futures, Many Worlds: Theme and Form in Science Fiction*. Ed. Thomas D. Clareson. Kent, OH: Kent UP, 1977. 182–223.
Wasserman, Robin. *Skinned*. New York: Simon and Schuster, 2008.
Wendell, Carolyn. "Miss Forsyte Is Dead—Long Live the Sci-Fi Lady!" *Teaching Science Fiction: Education for Tomorrow*. Ed. Jack Williamson. Philadelphia: Owlswick Press, 1980. 102–9.
Westerfeld, Scott. *Uglies*. New York: Simon and Schuster, 2005.
Weyn, Suzanne. *The Bar Code Tattoo*. New York: Scholastic, 2004.
Wiederhold, Eve. "Called to the Law: Tales of Pleasure and Obedience." *Rhetoric Review* 20.1/2 (2001): 130–46.
Williamson, Jack. "Introduction." *Teaching Science Fiction: Education for Tomorrow*. Ed. Jack Williamson. Philadelphia: Owlswick Press, 1980. 9–18.
Xiaolan, Wang. "Dystopian Nightmare in Contemporary Adolescent Fiction and Its Ethical Value." *Forum for World Literature Studies* 8.1 (2016): 75–86.
Zappen, James P. "Kenneth Burke on Dialectical-Rhetorical Transcendence." *Philosophy and Rhetoric* 42.3 (2009): 279–301.
Zipes, Jack. "Foreword: Utopia, Dystopia, and the Quest for Hope." *Utopian and Dystopian Writing for Children and Young Adults*. Ed. Carrie Hintz and Elaine Ostry. New York: Taylor and Francis Books, 2003. ix–xi.
Žižek, Slavoj. *The Plauge of Fantasies*. London: Verso, 1997.
Žižek, Slavoj. *The Žižek Reader*. Ed. Elizabeth Wright and Edmund Wright. Oxford, UK: Blackwell, 1999.
Žižek, Slavoj. *Revolution at the Gates*. London: Verso, 2002.

INDEX

47, 52, 53
1984, 7, 89, 92, 95, 107, 113, 117, 120, 144, 145, 146, 147, 165, 171. See also Orwell, George
2001: A Space Odyssey, 144
20,000 Leagues Under the Sea, 144. See also Verne, Jules

Abjection, 26, 27, 32, 33, 34, 170, 171
Adolescence, 5, 9, 32, 33, 34, 36; lit, 37, 38, 39, 40, 42, 44; literature, 56–57, 61, 63, 65, 71, 84–87, 88, 91, 93, 95, 96, 100, 106, 132, 137, 138, 149, 151, 155, 157, 158, 163, 170, 171, 173. See also Young adults
After Earth, 156 158, 159, 161, 163
Agamben, Georgio, 26, 27, 28, 37, 38, 113
Alexander, Jonathan, and Rebecca Black, 137, 138
Alien, 144, 151
Aliens, 30, 43, 48, 53, 59, 60, 72, 163
Althusser, Louis, 9, 10, 11, 12, 13, 14, 15, 16, 17, 18, 20, 21, 23, 36, 38, 57, 87, 169
Ames, Melissa A., 132, 133, 134, 148, 149
Ames, Mildred, 63. See also *Anna to the Infinite Power*

Among the Hidden, 4, 92, 93, 95. See also Haddix, Margaret Peterson
Anderson, Erland, 122, 125, 126
Anderson, M. T., 165, 166, 171, 175
Animal Farm, 91. See also Orwell, George
Anna to the Infinite Power, 63, 64, 65
Anthem, 89. See also Rand, Ayn
Armageddon 2419 AD, 172
Asimov, Isaac, 45, 46, 48, 171
Atlas Shrugged, 166
Atwood, Margaret, 79, 90, 152, 173. See also *Handmaid's Tale, The*

Baccolini, Rafaella, 39, 85
Barcode Tattoo, The, 93, 94
Bartter, Martha, 43
Basu, Balaka, 164
Baudrillard, Jean, 35, 75
Be More Chill, 51, 144. See also Vizzini, Ned
Beebee, Thomas O., 41, 42
Bixler, Andrea, 123
Blade Runner, 7, 165, 171, 175
Bloch, Ernst, 34, 50. See also *Novum*
Booker, M. Keith, 77, 78, 81

Bracher, Mark, 142
Bradbury, Ray, 89, 144
Bradford, Clare, Kerry Mallan, John Stephens, and Robyn McCallum, 81, 83, 85, 160
Brave New World, 89, 175, 176. See also Huxley, Aldous
Brazil, 144
Broad, Katherine R., 164. See also Basu, Balaka
Brown, Tom, 92
Bullen, Elizabeth, and Elizabeth Parsons, 39, 85
Burgess, Anthony, 89. See also *Wanting Seed, The*
Burke, Kenneth, 9, 15, 20, 23, 25, 26, 27, 34, 39, 44; Burkean identification, 24, 38, 60, 70, 85, 87, 170

Calkins, Elizabeth, and Barry McGhan, 139, 140
Callinicos, Alex, 11, 13, 14
Carter, C. Allen, 25, 27
Children of Men, The, 90
Childs, Ann M. M., 164
Chocolate War, The, 92, 107, 110, 114
Christopher, John, 92
City of Ember, The, 93, 173. See also DuPrau, Jeanne
Cixous, Hélène, 29
Clarke, Simon, 13
Clockwork Orange, A, 89
Coats, Karen, 26, 27, 28, 32, 33, 34, 56, 95, 100, 103, 170, 171
Coding, 35, 59, 63, 94, 154, 161, 170, 171
Cognitive estrangement, 34, 35, 50, 51, 58, 59, 61, 144, 170, 171
Cohn, Dorrit, 17, 19
Collins, Suzanne, 136. See also *Hunger Games, The*
Cormier, Robert, 92, 107, 110, 114
Couzelis, Mary J., 153
Cuarón, Alfonso, 90

Cure, The, 92
Cyberpunk, 46, 48, 165, 166, 171, 175; post-, 48, 171, 175

Dashner, James, 100, 136. See also *Maze Runner, The*
David Starr, Space Ranger, 48
Day the Earth Stood Still, The, 144
Daz 4 Zoe, 92
Dick, Philip K., 90
Divergent, 165
Donawerth, Jane, 124, 125, 126
Dream-weaver, 71, 72
Dubrow, Heather, 41
Duff, David, 40
DuPrau, Jeanne, 93, 97, 172, 173
Dystopias, 7, 38, 39, 40, 77, 78, 79, 81, 82, 83, 84, 85, 86, 88, 89, 90, 92, 93, 94, 96, 100, 107, 109, 110, 114, 116, 119, 129, 130, 131, 134, 136, 137, 138, 139, 144, 148, 149, 152, 153, 155, 156, 160, 163, 164, 165, 166, 172, 176
Dystopian literature, 3, 4, 5, 6, 9, 10, 17, 21, 23, 28, 31, 34, 37, 78, 81, 87, 91, 107, 117, 120, 125, 126, 127, 128, 130, 140, 141, 143, 144, 148; YA, 7, 40, 42, 80, 86, 92, 95, 113, 132, 133, 137, 139, 152, 153, 154, 156, 163, 164, 167, 168, 172, 173, 175, 176

Elliot, Amy, 136, 137
Enchantress from the Stars, 68. See also Engdahl, Sylvia
Engdahl, Sylvia, 68, 69, 70, 71, 72

Farenheit 451, 89, 144
Feed, 165, 166, 171, 175
Feldner, Heiko, 16, 17, 18, 19, 20, 22, 23
Feminism, 90; authors and critics of, 36, 54–55; scholars, 175; science fiction, 65
Fifth Element, The, 144
Forbidden Planet, 144
Foucault, Michel, 9, 15, 16, 17, 18, 19, 20, 21, 23, 27, 28, 33, 37, 38, 57, 87, 100, 169

Frank, Marietta, 38, 47, 58, 59, 82, 83, 84, 161, 162
Freedman, Carl, 34, 36, 37, 50, 56, 57, 74, 139, 140, 166, 171, 176
Freedman, Kerry, 139, 140
Freire, Paulo, 142
Futuretrack 5, 92

Gate to Women's Country, The, 90
George, Jean Craighead, 159. See also *My Side of the Mountain*
Giver, The, 84, 92, 93, 113, 116, 117, 144, 146, 173. See also Lowry, Lois
Godzich, Wlad, 30
Golding, William, 91. See also *Lord of the Flies*
Gordon, Joan, 60; and Veronica Hollinger, 43
Gordon, Neve, 19
Guardians, The, 92
Gunn, James, 121, 122

Haddix, Margaret Peterson, 4, 92, 95, 116. See also *Among the Hidden*
Handmaid's Tale, The, 79, 90, 152, 173
Hansel and Gretel, 172
Hanson, Carter F., 175
Harris-Fain, Darren, 43
Hatchet, 159, 163
Hatty, Suzanne E., 30, 60, 67
Have Spacesuit Will Travel, 144. See also Heinlein, Robert
Heinlein, Robert, 46, 48, 147, 175
Heinlein Juveniles, 48
Heller, Kevin Jon, 18, 19
Hintz, Carrie, 78, 79, 83, 84, 108, 116, 132, 153, 160, 164. See also Ostry, Elaine
Hollindale, Peter, 83
Homo Sacer, 26, 27, 38, 110, 113
hooks, bell, 141
Hughes, Monica, 92
Hunger Games, The, 134, 135, 137, 166
Huxley, Aldous, 89, 175

Identification, 10, 12, 21, 25, 67, 69, 70, 71, 93, 94, 95, 100, 104, 137; Burkean, 20, 23, 24, 38, 60, 70, 85, 87, 170; disidentification, 65, 85
Ideological State Apparatus (ISA), 5, 9, 11, 15, 17, 20, 23, 33, 80, 87, 93, 95, 96, 98, 100, 101, 109, 110, 111, 112, 113, 114, 115, 169
Ideology, 10, 11, 12, 13, 14, 15, 16, 18, 20, 21, 22, 23, 24, 36, 41, 42, 55, 58, 60, 69, 70, 75, 88, 89, 95, 100, 114, 125, 127, 143, 144, 146, 169, 170, 177, 178
Interpellation, 11, 12, 18, 23, 24, 28, 34, 37, 44
Iron Heel, The, 89
I Was a Teenage Popsicle, 57, 61. See also Rosenbaum, Bev Katz

James, P. D., 90
Jameson, Fredric, 38, 44, 79, 81, 107, 160, 163, 164, 170

Lacan, Jacques: psychoanalysis, 20; subject formation, 28, 29, 30, 170
Lawrence, Louise, 71
L'Engle, Madeleine, 48
Les Guérillères, 90
Levinas, 30, 31, 32, 170
Levitin, Sonia, 92
Littman, Sarah Darer, 135, 136, 175
Logan's Run, 90
London, Jack, 89
Longyear, Barry, 123
Looking Backward, 172
Lord of the Flies, 91, 135
Lovell, Terry, 14
Lowry, Lois, 84, 92, 93, 113, 114, 115, 117, 144, 146. See also *Giver, The*

Mannheim, Karl, 88
Maze Runner, The, 93, 100, 135, 136
McDonnell, Kevin, and Kevin Robins, 13, 14

McKay, George, 127
Mendlesohn, Farah, 49, 50, 55, 60
Middle School: The Worst Years of My Life, 176
Mikaelsen, Ben, 159. See also *Touching Spirit Bear*
"Minority Report, The," 90
Molson, Francis J., 45, 47, 170
Montag, Warren, 13, 15
Mosley, Walter, 52. See also 47
Moylan, Tom, 80, 172
My Side of the Mountain, 159, 163
My Teacher Is an Alien, 171

Nama, Adilufu, 154
Natfact 7, 92
News from Nowhere, 172
Nodal Point, 117
Nodelman, Perry, 40
Nolan, William F., 90
Novum, 34, 50, 52, 53, 56, 58, 71, 74, 172

O/other, the, 4, 6, 9, 10, 29, 30, 31, 32, 33, 35, 42, 44, 49, 59, 60, 62, 63, 64, 65, 66, 67, 69, 73, 74, 127, 144, 147, 154, 170, 171
Orwell, George, 81, 82, 89, 91, 95, 107, 113, 117, 144, 145, 146, 165. See also *1984*
Ostry, Elaine, 61, 65, 78, 79, 83, 84, 108, 116, 153, 160. See also Hintz, Carrie
Othering, 4, 6, 31, 34, 35, 44, 49, 51, 59, 60, 63, 64, 67, 68, 69, 71, 72, 73, 74, 75, 77, 147

Panopticon, 27, 28, 37, 105, 106
Parrinder, Patrick, 120, 121, 129, 174
Patterson, James, 176
Paulsen, Gary, 159. See also *Hatchet*
Plank, Robert, 131
Plato, 88, 89
Posthumanism, 48, 61, 65
Power, 4, 6, 7, 11, 15, 16, 17, 18, 19, 20, 21, 23, 25, 27, 29, 31; and the adolescent, 32–33, 34, 37, 38, 39, 47, 51, 57, 66, 67, 73; and the child, 86, 87, 88, 92; classroom, 141, 142, 145, 147, 168, 169, 170; disempowering, 74, 77, 81, 82, 83, 84, 85; empowered, 36, 126, 142, 159; and healing of trauma, 137, 139; ISA, 94–95, 96, 97, 99, 108, 109, 110, 128, 129, 130, 135

Rand, Ayn, 89, 166. See also *Atlas Shrugged*
Ratcliffe, Krista, 24, 25
Red Zone, 92
Reed, Kit, 90
Reeves, Keanu, 52, 171
Reid, Suzanne Elizabeth, 46
Repression, 16, 18, 39, 57, 88
Repressive State Apparatus (RSA), 5, 9, 10, 11, 15, 17, 80, 93, 95, 97, 98, 99, 100, 111, 113, 169
Republic, 88. See also Plato
Reynolds, Kimberly, 134, 139
Reznor, Trent, 91
Robbie, 171. See also Asimov, Isaac
Roberts, Adam, 35, 43, 48, 49, 59, 75
Roccanti, Rikki, 126, 127
Rocket Ship Galileo, 48. See also Heinlein, Robert
Rodden, John, 120, 173, 174
Roemer, Kenneth M., 130, 131
Rosenbaum, Bev Katz, 61, 172. See also *I Was a Teenage Popsicle*
Rybakova, Katie, 126, 127

Sagan, Carl, 123
Sambell, Kay, 84, 85, 86, 132, 133, 172
Sands, Karen, 38, 47, 58, 59, 82, 83, 84, 161, 162
Sargent, Lymon Tower, 80
Scholes, Robert, 106, 107, 174
Science fiction, 3, 4, 5, 6, 7, 9, 10, 17, 21, 44, 45, 130, 165; authors of, 51, 54, 55, 56, 57, 58, 59, 60, 61, 65, 67, 74, 75, 77, 81, 86, 87, 91, 92, 106, 107, 110, 116, 117, 119, 120, 121, 122; consumers of, 23,

30, 32, 34, 35, 36, 37, 42, 43; history of, 46, 47, 48; as mode, 49, 50; pedagogy of, 123, 124, 125, 126, 127, 128, 129, 131, 137, 140, 141, 143, 144, 147, 151, 152, 154, 155, 156, 157, 160, 161, 162, 163, 166, 167, 168, 170, 171, 172, 173, 174, 176; speculative fiction and, 44, 45; YA, 44, 50, 55, 56, 74, 127, 144, 152, 154, 163
Scott, Ridley, 151
Sex Offender, The, 90
Seymour, Jessica, 134, 135
Shusterman, Neal, 104, 105, 126. See also *Unwind*
Simulacra, 35, 75
Skinned, 65, 73
Sleeping Beauty, 172
Smith, Jaden, 157
Smith, Will, 157, 158
Space Opera, 172
Spielberg, Steven, 90
Spirited Away, 172
Stadler, Matthew, 90
Stargate, 144
Star Trek, 46, 151, 175
Steele, Meili, 23
Steward, Susan, 164
Stranger in a Strange Land, 125, 147, 175. See also Heinlein, Robert
Strasser, Todd, 92, 107, 108. See also *Wave, The*
Subjectivity, 4, 10, 12, 15, 17, 18, 20, 24, 28, 29, 30, 31, 32, 35, 36, 38, 42, 66, 68, 75, 78, 79, 80, 85, 86, 95, 105, 111, 113, 161, 168, 169, 173, 174
Sullivan, C.W., III, 44
Surveillance, 15, 34, 37, 39, 57, 84, 88, 90, 93, 100, 102, 105, 107, 108, 139, 156; Foucauldian, 19, 20, 38, 87; normative, 16, 19, 20
Susina, Jan, 155
Suvin, Darko, 34, 50, 161, 170
Svilpis, Jānis, 47
Swindel, Robert, 92

Teenagers, 33; literature, 47, 68, 84
Tepper, Sherri S., 90
Thinner Than Thou, 90
THX 1138, 90, 144
Time Machine, The, 166. See also Wells, H. G.
Todorov, Tzvetan, 41
Tom Swift, 47
Tomorrow City, The, 92
Touching Spirit Bear, 159, 163
Toumayan, Alain P., 31, 170
Trans-ideological kernel, 20, 21, 38
Trites, Roberta Seelinger, 33, 34, 36, 37, 39, 40, 56, 57, 67, 87, 88, 96, 100, 103, 169
Tully, John, 92

Uglies, 93, 95. See also Westerfeld, Scott
Unwind, 93, 126, 152
Unwind, 104, 105, 106. See also Shusterman, Neal
Unwinding, 104, 105, 106, 173
Use value (of genre), 5, 40, 41, 42, 45, 79, 82, 108, 116, 122, 123, 126, 127, 133, 167. See also Beebee, Thomas
Utopias, 6, 13, 23, 38, 39, 77, 78, 79, 81, 82, 83, 84, 85, 88, 89, 92, 97, 108, 109, 114, 115, 116, 124, 144, 146, 160, 172, 174; literature, 153

Verne, Jules, 144, 171
Vighi, Fabio, 16, 17, 18, 19, 20, 22, 23
Vizzini, Ned, 51, 144, 171

Wanting Seed, The, 90. See also Burgess, Anthony
Warrick, Patricia, 83
Wasserman, Robin, 65. See also *Skinned*
Watership Down, 91
Wave, The, 92, 107, 108, 109
We, 89
Wells, H. G., 89, 90. See also *Time Machine, The*
Wendell, Carolyn, 121

Westall, Robert, 92. See also *Futuretrack 5*
Westerfeld, Scott, 93, 95, 172
Weyn, Suzanne, 93. See also *Barcode Tattoo, The*
Wiederhold, Eve, 12
Williamson, Jack, 120, 122, 174
Wittig, Monique, 90
Wrinkle in Time, A, 48

Xiaolan, Wang, 77, 138, 139

"Year Zero," 91
Young adults (YA), 5, 6, 7, 9, 10, 28, 32, 33, 34, 36, 37, 39, 40, 43, 44, 45, 46, 47, 48, 49, 50, 51, 52, 53, 54, 55, 56, 57, 58, 59, 60, 61, 63, 64, 65, 66, 67, 68, 69, 70, 71, 72, 73, 74, 75, 77, 78, 80, 81, 83, 88, 91, 92, 95, 96, 126, 127, 132, 133, 137, 140, 148, 151, 152, 153, 154, 156, 159, 162, 167, 168, 169, 170, 171, 172, 173, 174, 175, 176
Young adult science fiction, 9, 34, 36, 44, 55, 56, 74, 140, 162, 167

Zamyatin, Yevgeny, 89
Zipes, Jack, 78, 80, 86
Žižek, Slavoj, 14, 20, 21, 22, 35, 38, 70, 75, 160, 163

ABOUT THE AUTHOR

Photo by Audrey Jeans of Audie Jeans Photography

Joseph Campbell received his master's in literature from University of South Alabama, and his PhD from Illinois State University. He teaches English at Casper College in Casper, Wyoming.

www.ingramcontent.com/pod-product-compliance
Lightning Source LLC
Chambersburg PA
CBHW030624230426
43661CB00053B/2135